50

key
concepts in
theology

Also by Hugh Rayment-Pickard

The Devil's Account: Philip Pullman and Christianity
The Myths of Time: From Saint Augustine to American Beauty

50

key concepts in theology

Hugh Rayment-Pickard

DARTON·LONGMAN + TODD

for Rachel Carr

First published in 2007 by
Darton, Longman and Todd Ltd
1 Spencer Court
140–142 Wandsworth High Street
London SW18 4JJ

ISBN-10 0-232-52622-2
ISBN-13 978-0-232-52622-6

A catalogue record for this book is available from the British Library.

Designed and produced by Sandie Boccacci
Set in 10.5/13pt Minion
Printed and bound in Great Britain by
Cromwell Press, Trowbridge, Wiltshire

Contents

Preface

This book is intended to be both useful and interesting. Theology, like any other discipline, has its own jargon and insider knowledge. People often ask me questions like: What's 'narrative theology'? Or, What exactly is 'post-modern theology'? I thought there was a place for a book that provided some digestible answers to these questions. And in order to make the entries more engaging, they contain comment and opinion as well as description.

Although there are only 50 main sections, each section contains many shorter references to thinkers, ideas and books. So the book as a whole has several hundred entries.

This book doesn't pretend to be comprehensive and it is best to think of it as a collection of short essays on some key topics in theology. The range of themes and thinkers is not exhaustive and inevitably follows my own interests. The choice of topics will certainly not please everyone, and to those readers I can only offer Dr Johnson's words as an advance apology: 'Dictionaries are like watches; the worst is better than none, and the best cannot be expected to go quite true.'

I am grateful once again to Rachel Carr ('the world's greatest proof-reader') to whom this book is dedicated, for taking such meticulous care in commenting on the text.

HUGH RAYMENT-PICKARD
Notting Hill, 2006

Atheism

The conviction that God does not exist.

In the ancient world the word 'atheist' tended to be used to describe those who failed to believe in particular gods. Epicurus, Democritus and Lucretius were regarded as atheists because they challenged certain theistic ideas, but they did not reject all possibility of divine existence. It is not until the modern period that 'atheism' becomes a distinctive and widespread philosophical position.

The history of modern atheism begins in the Enlightenment, with many different kinds of argument being launched against belief in God. David Hume, a Scottish philosopher, offered a rational critique, arguing that the world around us does not offer definite evidence of God's existence. There were moral objections – for example, from D'Holbach – to belief in a bloodthirsty God who punishes people by burning them eternally in hell. Ludwig Feuerbach offered a psychological argument for atheism, saying that God is only a projection of our inner human need for meaning. Nietzsche argued that belief in God is an illusion that inhibits 'the will to life'. Karl Marx offered a political critique of theism, saying that belief in God is a drug ('the opium of the people') that deadens our desire to fight for justice. Sigmund Freud argued that belief in God is a cultural projection of our need for a 'father figure' to protect us from the hostile forces of nature.

The philosophical difficulty with atheism is that it is defined by what it is against rather than by what it believes. So it is no more possible to speak about the positive content of atheism than it is possible to speak about the positive content of 'not being English' or 'not being a fish'. There are also numerous possible conceptions of God, so a total atheist position would have to supply an exhaustive list of all the gods that are not believed in.

And there is a logical paradox at the heart of atheism: it requires the concept of God in order to define itself, so to some extent atheists give credence to the gods they are against precisely by pointing out their non-existence. If there were a campaign to show that the man on the moon doesn't exist, it would automatically give status to the counter-claim that the man on the moon is in fact alive and well. A perfect atheism would have to pass beyond disbelief to a complete indifference to the question of God's existence.

Many atheists have not reached this point of equanimity and rail with an almost religious zeal against God – for example, the Darwinian, Richard Dawkins. It is often said that atheism is just another faith and that there are no better grounds for atheism than theism. It is argued that atheism is just another religion, but a self-deceiving one, because it never admits its own dimension of faith – that is, the faith that God does not exist.

The 2001 UK census recorded that 15.1 per cent of the population are non-religious. After 200 years of scientific and cultural critique of theism, this is a rather unimpressive statistic. The more remarkable fact is that so many people still believe in God (nearly 77 per cent according to the 2001 census) after so many decades of secular criticism and indifference.

THINKERS

Richard Dawkins (1941–) argues passionately that belief in God is an irrational delusion and that religions are dangerous.

Democritus (460–370 BC) argued that the universe is made up of material atoms and denied the existence of spiritual substances.

Epicurus (341–270 BC) was a materialist who argued that the universe consists only of matter and the spaces between matter.

Ludwig Feuerbach (1804–72) argued in *The Essence of Christianity* (1841) that God is a human projection: 'The divine being is nothing else than the human being, or rather, human nature purified … made objective, that is, contemplated and revered as another, a distinct being.'

Sigmund Freud (1856–1939) wrote in *Civilization and its Discontents* (1930) that religion 'is so patently infantile, so foreign to reality, that to anyone with a friendly attitude to humanity it is painful to think that the majority of mortals will never be able to rise above this view of life.'

James Froude (1818–94) offered a moral argument against a vengeful God: 'I would sooner perish for ever than stoop down before a Being who may have power to crush me, but whom my heart forbids me to reverence.'

Baron D'Holbach (1723–89) argued that the gods of religion were barbaric and that human beings were morally superior to God: 'The Jehovah of the Jews is a suspicious tyrant ... The pure mind of the Christians resolved, in order to appease his fury, to crucify his own son.'

George Holyoake (1817–1906) was the last person in England to be criminally punished for atheism. He was jailed for six months in 1842. (See also 'Secularisation'.)

David Hume (1711–76): although there is some debate about whether Hume was an atheist, he is normally taken for one, and he did criticise many aspects of theistic belief.

Lucretius (99–55 BC) argued that belief in gods is not necessary or likely to bring about happiness: 'Fear holds dominion over mortality only because, seeing in land and sky so much the cause whereof no wise they know, men think divinities are working there.'

Justyn Martyr (100–165), in his *First Apology*, agreed with the Roman accusation that Christians were atheists: 'We do confess ourselves atheists before those whom you regard as gods, but not with respect to the Most True God.'

Philip Pullman (1946–) argues that belief in God diminishes human moral dignity and leads to oppressive religions.

Socrates (470–399 BC), at his trial, was accused of not believing in any kind of god, and offered the defence that he believed in other gods.

François-Marie Voltaire (1694–1778), like many of the Enlightenment *philosophes*, regarded belief in God as inherently dangerous: 'Fanaticism is certainly a thousand times more deadly; for atheism inspires no bloody passion.'

IDEAS

Methodical atheism: the refusal by scientists to use God as a short-cut to provide explanations. Even believing scientists generally search first for natural explanations, as if there were no God.

Non-cognitivism: the view that religious and ethical beliefs are expressions of human feeling rather than statements about the objective truth.

Occam's Razor: the principle, devised by William of Occam

(1288–1348), that 'entities should not be multiplied beyond necessity', which could be used to argue that God is an unnecessary idea.

Scepticism: the tendency to doubt.

BOOKS

Michael J. Buckley, *At the Origins of Modern Atheism* (Yale, 1987)

Robin Le Poidevin, *Arguing for Atheism* (Routledge, 1996)

Alasdair MacIntyre and Paul Ricoeur, *The Religious Significance of Atheism* (Columbia, 1966)

Alister McGrath, *The Twilight of Atheism: The Rise and Fall of Disbelief in the Modern World* (Doubleday, 2004)

Atonement

Atonement is the 'at-one-ment' or 'reconciliation' of God with humanity achieved by Christ's death upon the cross.

The classical doctrine of the atonement depends upon the doctrine of the fall, which says that humanity has become alienated from God through human sinfulness. The doctrine of the atonement says that Christ's death somehow – the 'somehow' being a matter of much dispute – reconciled humanity with God.

The history of the doctrine of the atonement is instructive. All doctrines have an evolutionary history as ideas develop and culture changes. The earliest doctrines of the atonement – which were the orthodoxy of their time – have long since been superseded. Indeed, the doctrine of the atonement is still a matter of fierce debate.

The earliest doctrines of the atonement, prevalent among the Church Fathers and in the centuries up to the first millennium, were so-called 'victory' or 'ransom' theories. The world was believed to be under the control of the devil, who demanded Jesus' death as the price for releasing humanity from its satanic captivity. These ideas of 'ransom', 'hostage' and 'captivity' persist in our Easter hymns. But there is something unsatisfactory about the idea that God does deals with the devil. This was pointed out both by Peter Abelard and by St Anselm, who said that the ransom theory implied that the devil had rights or powers that God had to respect. And this was clearly not acceptable.

It was St Anselm, writing a thousand years after the birth of Christianity, who proposed a revised understanding of the atonement, offering a new theory based upon God's need to punish someone for the sins of humanity. Anselm's argument is that human sinfulness requires some kind of divine punishment. But God's mercy prevents him from punishing us, so Jesus offers himself as our 'substitute', taking the blame on our behalf. Thus God squares the circle by remaining both fully just and fully merciful.

There is, as Peter Abelard first pointed out in the twelfth century, something repellent about the punishment theory of the atonement:

> How cruel and wicked it seems that anyone should demand the blood of an innocent person as the price for anything, or that it should in any way please him that an innocent man should be slain – still less that God should consider the death of his Son so agreeable that by it he should be reconciled to the whole world!

Abelard proposed an alternative 'exemplar theory' of the atonement, arguing that Jesus' death on the cross provided us with a life-changing example of stoical love in the face of injustice, cruelty, violence and death. Christ's death showed us the way out of sin and the path back to reconciliation with God. Abelard's version of the atonement has recently been championed by René Girard, who rejects penal substitution, seeing it as a form of scapegoating. Girard argues that Jesus made a self-sacrifice of his life to show precisely that there is a non-violent alternative to scapegoating. Since we are, Girard says, creatures who learn by imitating others, Jesus' death is a virtuous example that can bring about social transformation.

The problem with exemplar theories – most 'solutions' also create new problems – is that they do not clearly explain how Christ's heroic and exemplary death achieves the objective of cancelling the historic sins of humanity. A more radical solution is to re-think the atonement altogether and detach it from the event of the crucifixion. It is possible to argue (see Michael Winter, *The Atonement*, 1995) that the atonement comes about through the Last Supper and the Eucharist, as Jesus gives himself to us as a spiritual resource. Winter argues that Jesus did not 'die for our sins' but endured a martyr's death, refusing to capitulate in the face of earthly power and violence.

Anselm's doctrine is increasingly an embarrassment to Christian theology. As Girard comments, penal substitution 'has done more than anything else to discredit Christianity in the eyes of the modern world' (*Things hidden since the foundation of the world*, 1987). A theological logic of crime and punishment, that worked for a previous epoch, now looks barbaric and paints God as a monster. One of the features of Christian theology in the twenty-first century will be the gradual abandonment of the penal view of the atonement in favour of non-violent alternatives. Perhaps some of these alternatives have still to be thought up.

Some traditionalists are concerned already about what they call the 'downgrading' of Anselm's doctrine of atonement. But the fact that Anselm's 'penal substitution' theory of the atonement, or versions of it, only became orthodoxy after a thousand years of Christianity, shows that the Christian idea of truth is subject to radical change. Today's orthodoxy may well be tomorrow's heresy, and vice versa.

THINKERS

Peter Abelard (1079–1142) argued that Christ's death merely showed us the way to the atonement.

St Anselm (c. 1033–1109) developed the classic view that God has to demand satisfaction for the dishonour brought upon him by human sin. Christ's death satisfies God's honour because it is the sacrifice of a perfect human being.

Gustav Aulén (1879–1977) tried to rehabilitate the view of the Early Fathers that the atonement must be understood as part of a theological drama in which Jesus 'defeats' the powers of evil (*Christus Victor*, 1931).

René Girard (1923–) rejects any idea of a violent father punishing his son on the cross. Girard sees the death of Jesus as an exemplary, non-violent act of turning the other cheek.

St Paul (3–65) argued that Jesus' death reconciled us to God 'once and for all' by destroying the power of sin.

Karl Rahner (1904–84) argued that Jesus' death is 'an efficacious sign of the redeeming love that communicates God himself, because the cross establishes God's love in the world in a definitive and historically irreversible way' (*Theological Investigations*, chapter 21).

Albrecht Ritschl (1822–89), a liberal theologian, argued that the atonement is moral and spiritual and concerns an inner change in the believer.

Thomas Szasz (1920–), a psychologist, argued that 'in the rejection, or transcending, of the scapegoat principle lies the greatest moral challenge for modern man. On its resolution may hinge the fate of our species' (*The Manufacture of Madness*).

IDEAS

Limited atonement: the belief that God is only reconciled to those who have been predestined for salvation.

Penal substitution: the idea that Jesus accepts a death penalty that is rightly ours because of our sin.

Propitiation: the idea that God must be appeased because of the wrong done to him by human beings.

Ransom theory: this theory of the atonement states that Christ's life was a ransom paid to the devil in order to save humanity.

The Suffering Servant: a figure in the book of Isaiah (chapter 53), often taken to be a reference to Christ, who is 'wounded for our transgressions'.

Sacrifice: the idea that Jesus sacrifices his life for the 'higher' cause of saving humanity.

Socinianism: the Socinians (followers of Faustus Socinius in the sixteenth century) argued that Christ did not die for our sins. God is perfectly benevolent and could never sanction the crucifixion. So Christ's death was merely an example to us of perfect forgiveness.

BOOKS

Colin Gunton, *The Actuality of Atonement: A Study of Metaphor, Rationality and the Christian Tradition* (Eerdmans, 1989)

Paul Fiddes, *Past Event and Present Salvation: The Christian Idea of Atonement* (Westminster/John Knox Press, 1989)

Biblical Criticism

**The application of various textual and histori-
cal methods to the books of the Bible.**

The critical examination of Scripture is a product of the modern
period and has its roots in the development of a new historical consciousness in the late eighteenth century. Thinkers started to become
more aware that religions have a history, and that even religious texts
are produced within distinct cultural settings. And so biblical
scholars (almost all of them German) started to ask about the history
of the production of the biblical texts: who wrote them, why they
were written, and who were they written for.

The impulse of the first modern biblical critics was not essentially
religious but historical. Their goal was to elicit the historical truth of
Scripture rather than any divine meaning or message. David Strauss
(one of the first modern biblical critics) suggested that the miraculous parts of the Gospels might just be myths. Before this time
'rationalist' critics had tied themselves in knots trying to devise
ordinary explanations for the miracles. Strauss reached the more
audacious conclusion that many parts of Jesus' life were simply made
up by the early Church.

Strauss used biblical criticism to deconstruct the historical truth
of Jesus. But most eighteenth- and nineteenth-century scholars used
the tools of criticism to construct a 'true' factual story of Jesus: the so-
called 'historical Jesus'. The historical life of Jesus became a cultural
obsession: between 1800 and 1900 no less than 60,000 'lives of Jesus'
were published in Europe. Inevitably, each generation tended to produce a Jesus in its own image. The eighteenth-century rationalists
produced a rational Jesus who came to enlighten his people. The
nineteenth-century liberal Protestants produced an ethical Jesus who
came to show us how to live.

The magisterial figure in biblical criticism – even to this day – is
Albert Schweitzer. In *The Quest for the Historical Jesus* he crowned
and surpassed his predecessors by offering a convincing portrait of
Jesus as a Jewish eschatological prophet from an age quite unlike our
own. Schweitzer's book begged the question of the relevance of an

eschatological Jesus to the modern world, and Schweitzer concluded that the historical Jesus is 'a stranger to our time' but that his spiritual message is as relevant now as it was to the first disciples.

In exposing the strangeness of Jesus, Schweitzer set the tone for twentieth-century biblical scholarship, which focused upon Jesus' Jewish identity and painted a picture of him that was often starkly at odds with the Church's view. Critics questioned whether Jesus ever believed himself to be the Messiah, the truth of the miracles and even the historical existence of Jesus.

THINKERS

Rudolf Bultmann (1884–1976) argued that 'we can know almost nothing concerning the life and personality of Jesus since the Christian sources show no interest in either, are moreover fragmentary and often legendary; and other sources about Jesus do not exist.' The significant fact about Jesus, argued Bultmann, is his existentialist teaching (or *kerygma*), not the story of his life, which is a mere legend.

Johann Gottfried Eichhorn (1752–1827), a German biblical scholar, wrote introductions to both the Old and the New Testaments questioning the authenticity of particular biblical texts and developing theory about the sources of the Gospels.

Hermann Reimarus (1694–1758), a Deist, published the first modern historical study of Jesus' life, *The Aim of Jesus and His Disciples* (1778).

Albert Schweitzer (1875–1965) wrote *The Quest of the Historical Jesus* (1906), which was both the culmination of nineteenth-century historical criticism and the beginning of new historical–critical study in the twentieth century.

D. F. Strauss (1808–74) published *The Life of Jesus Critically Examined* (1835). Strauss argued that 'it was time to substitute a new mode of considering the life of Jesus, in the place of the antiquated systems of supranaturalism and naturalism … every part of [the history of Jesus] is to be subjected to a critical examination, to ascertain whether it have not some admixture of the mythical.' One reviewer called *The Life* 'the most pestilential book ever vomited out of the jaws of hell'. The book was translated into English by the novelist George Eliot.

IDEAS

Allegory: allegories are stories in which the events and characters have a higher symbolic significance.

Demythologisation: an approach pioneered by Rudolf Bultmann which attempted to show (1) that most of the New Testament and its thought-world is mythical; and (2) that the biblical myths must be reinterpreted if we are to apply them to our modern existence.

Double dissimilarity: the idea, put forward by Bultmann, that if any given saying of Jesus bore similarity to any other Jewish or Christian sources, it should be disregarded as inauthentic. Only those sayings dissimilar both to Jewish and early Christian culture should be regarded as Jesus' own words.

Eisegesis: the interpretation of a text by 'reading in' or imposing a particular meaning.

Exegesis: the interpretation of a text by drawing out its inherent meaning.

Form Criticism: a misleading translation of the original German term *Formgeschichte*, which means 'history of form'. Form Criticism is the analysis of the history of the literary 'forms' out of which the Bible is structured. Form Criticism identifies the 'type' or 'form' (*Gattung*) of a biblical passage, and tries to determine the social and historical circumstances (*Sitz im Leben*) which gave rise to that 'type' or 'form'.

Genre Criticism: analyses the literary genres of the biblical texts, and what influence the genre of a specific text should have upon its interpretation.

Hexapla: the name given to Origen's edition of the Old Testament in Hebrew and Greek – the first work of Christian textual criticism (second century AD).

Higher Criticism: the term coined by Eichhorn for the examination of the themes, structures and meanings of Scripture.

The Jesus Seminar: convened in 1985 to determine, verse by verse through the Gospels, which words of Jesus were historical.

Lower Criticism: another term for Textual Criticism.

The Principle of Accommodation: devised by Matthew Arnold, this argued that an infinite and supreme being must 'accommodate' his message, putting it into anthropological terms, in order for it to be understood by puny human beings. Arnold said (in 'On the Right Interpretation of the Scriptures') that terms such as the 'hands', 'eyes' and 'ears' of God are surely 'accommodations'.

Q (or Quelle): a hypothetical book of sayings of Jesus that may have been used by Matthew and Luke in the writing of their Gospels.

Redaction Criticism: analyses the work and beliefs of the editors of Scripture, trying to discern their purposes, attitudes and concerns. Modern New Testament Redaction Criticism has focused upon the Gospel writers as editors of received sources and traditions.

Source Criticism: the attempt to discern the sources of information, stories and sayings which have been used in the writing of the biblical texts. The classic Source-Critical study of the Old Testament is the spectacular Graf-Wellhausen 'document' theory of the Pentateuch. This theory detected four distinct sources which contributed to the Pentateuch as we have it.

The Synoptic Problem: the question of the historical and literary relationship between the first three Gospels – the order and circumstances under which each was written. The dominant theory is the 'two-source hypothesis', which argues that the majority of the synoptic material derives from Mark's Gospel and a document called 'Q'.

Textual Criticism: this undertakes a word-by-word analysis of the various historical versions of the biblical texts. This involves a detailed knowledge of biblical languages such as Hebrew, Greek and Syriac.

The Intentional Fallacy: the supposedly fallacious belief that the meaning of a text is primarily that which the author intended.

Typology: this sees the persons, places and events of the Old Testament as 'types' which re-occur in the New Testament. St Paul uses a typological approach when he sees Adam as prefiguring Christ (Rom. 5:15–21) and when he refers to the Red Sea and baptism (1 Cor. 10:1–6).

BOOKS

John Barton (ed.), *The Cambridge Companion to Biblical Interpretation* (CUP, 1998)

Steve Moyise, *Introduction to Biblical Studies* (Continuum, 1998)

Christology

The study of Jesus' identity as Christ, the Messiah.

Christians believe that Jesus was not only human, but a divine Messiah or Christ (literally, 'the anointed one') with the power to save humanity. The study of Christ is called 'Christology'.

The debate about Jesus' christological identity starts in the Gospels. The Jews of Jesus' time expected the arrival of a Messiah. We see evidence of this expectation when both John the Baptist and Jesus are asked whether they are the Christ. But Jesus spoke evasively about himself as the Christ and discouraged his disciples from talking too openly about it. Jesus most commonly refers to himself as 'the Son of Man', an ambiguous title which may refer back to a messianic phrase in the book of Daniel, but is not obviously christological. The disciples appear to have treated Jesus as the Christ, referring to him not only as 'Lord' (*kyrios*) but as 'the Lord'.

For St Paul and the earliest Church, Jesus' christological status appears to have been neither controversial nor theologically problematic. But the paradox of the man who was God soon started to puzzle theologians. The problem was how one person could be both a creature and the creator, the divine source of everything and a carpenter in first-century Palestine.

The simplest solution to the problem was to argue, as the Docetists did, that Jesus only *appeared* to be human, that he was a God who wore his humanity like a garment – as it says in the famous carol, 'veiled in flesh the Godhead see'. Alternatively, one could argue, as Arius did, that Jesus was just a very special being, with a unique relationship with God. These, and other reductionist solutions, were eventually rejected by the churches at the Council of Chaldecon (451), which affirmed that Christ was fully human and fully divine.

Before the modern period, theologians made no real distinction between Jesus the human being and Christ the Messiah: Jesus was Christ, Christ was Jesus. But from the eighteenth century onwards there was a growing awareness both of human history and of the geological history of the planet. As a result, biblical scholars started to study Jesus as a historical figure like any other. This involved stripping him of his christological trappings in order to reveal Jesus the 'real' human being.

This produced various liberal christologies that saw Jesus as a more human figure – an ethical teacher rather than a cosmic, divine Messiah. These theologies argued the 'kenotic' view that Christ 'emptied himself' of his divinity in order to live just like us. The idea that Jesus swapped his divinity for humanity was a tidy, if not altogether satisfactory, solution to the age-old christological conundrum.

A number of twentieth-century theologians – D. M. Baillie and Dietrich Bonhoeffer, for example – argued that the paradox of christology is not a problem but is the structure of an alternative divine rationality which cannot be prised open by our human logic. If this is correct, then there will be no end to christological debate, because no christology will ever be adequate to 'solve' the puzzle of Christ's two natures.

In the 1970s and 1980s radical theologians started to voice explicitly a thought that had been lingering in theological circles for some time: that Jesus might really just have thought of himself as a human being with a remarkable character and message. John Hick, for example, edited a volume called *The Myth of God Incarnate* that claimed that 'the historical Jesus did not present Himself as God incarnate' and that the doctrine of the Trinity was invented by Church theologians.

The very open-endedness of Christ's identity is perhaps significant, meaning that he can never be reduced to our doctrines about him. The issue of Christ's identity invites theological curiosity as much now as it did for the first disciples.

THINKERS

St Anselm (1033–1109) argued that Christ's identity was centred upon his atoning work on the cross. (See 'Atonement'.)

D. M. Baillie (1887–1954) argued that Christ's nature is inherently paradoxical and that 'this paradox in its fragmentary form in our Christian lives is a reflection of that perfect union of God and man in the Incarnation on which the Christian life depends, and may therefore be our best clue to the understanding of it' (*God was in Christ*).

Marcus Borg (1942–) argues for a modern form of Arianism, saying that Jesus was a person with a very special sensitivity to God.

Pierre Teilhard de Chardin (1881–1955) saw Christ as a cosmic figure guiding the fragments and processes of the universe towards unification in a time of fulfilment and atonement that he called 'the omega point'.

Paul Tillich (1886–1965) argued that Jesus is an existential Christ who enables us to come to terms with our existential estrangement.

IDEAS

Arianism: the heresy named after its leader, Arius, who said Jesus was a higher being, but not God.

'Benefits' christology: the argument that we know Christ through the 'benefit' of the salvation that he won for us on the cross. It was summed up by Philip Melanchthon: 'to know Christ is to know his benefits.'

The Black Christ: the assertion that Christ was black and not the fair-haired white man of Western Christian tradition. Albert Cleage, for example, argued that Jesus should be seen as a Black Messiah with a particular relevance for black people.

Christa: the image of a female Christ used by some feminist theologians (for example, Carter Heyward).

The Council of Chalcedon in 451 settled the question of Jesus' divinity and humanity in the following formula (the so-called 'Chalcedonian definition'): Christ is 'truly God and truly man … one and the same Christ, Son, Lord, unique: acknowledged in two natures without confusion, without change, without division, without separation'. Critics have argued that this definition merely re-stated the problem, rather than explaining how the two natures of Christ are possible.

Docetism: the belief that Jesus was God disguised as a human.

Incarnation: a term derived from the Latin for 'to enflesh'. The incarnation is the doctrine that God 'took flesh' to become a human being in Jesus Christ.

Monophysitism: the view that Christ has only one nature – either human or divine.

Kenosis: the idea, derived from the letter to the Philippians (2:6–8), that Jesus 'emptied himself' of his divine nature in order to be human: 'though [Jesus] was in the form of God, [he] did not count equality with God a thing to be grasped, but emptied himself, taking the form of a servant, being born in the likeness of men. And being found in human form he humbled himself and became obedient unto death.'

The messianic secret: the intriguing phenomenon in Mark's Gospel where Jesus appears to keep his christological identity a secret (see for example, Mark 7:36).

The Myth of God Incarnate: the title of a collection of essays, published in 1977, that drew considerable attention, and criticism, for suggesting that Jesus was not God.

The speculative Christ: Hegel's idea that the truth of Christ lies in his eternal spiritual significance rather than in his historical identity. Hegel's use of the term 'speculative' is distinctive, meaning the spiritual dimension that transcends the particularity of time.

BOOKS

Kelly Brown Douglass, *The Black Christ* (Orbis Books, 1994)

Gerald O'Collins, *Christology: A Biblical, Historical and Systematic Study of Jesus Christ* (Oxford University Press, 1995)

John McQuarrie, *Jesus Christ in Modern Thought* (SCM, 1990)

Creation

The view of the world as having been made by God.

The very existence of the world provokes an obvious question: 'Where did all this stuff come from?' Or, put in its existentialist form: 'Why is there something rather than nothing?' The Christian answer to this question is that the world has a benevolent creator who created an orderly world for us to inhabit. This view has been under threat for some time from an atheistic–scientific view that the universe came into existence by itself, unaided by any supernatural being.

The Church Fathers, who set out the framework of creation theology, insisted on two key points: (1) Arguing against some classical assumptions about the eternity of the universe, Irenaeus and others made the case that the universe had a datable beginning in God's act of creation and that God created the world out of nothing (*ex nihilo*); (2) Arguing against the Gnostic view that there are two types of creation (good and bad) and two types of creator (benevolent and evil), Irenaeus and Augustine made the case that there is only one benevolent creator and that everything he created is good.

When we think about it, there is something audacious about the idea that everything has been created good. The world is manifestly imperfect – full of suffering, violence and injustice. But the Church Fathers were insistent that God can only create good things, and that there is only one God. This left the problem of how to explain evil. The solution adopted by Augustine, and later defended by Aquinas, was to offer another audacious argument: that evil does not exist. What we call 'evil' is merely the absence of goodness.

Since the mid-nineteenth century, the literal understanding of the Genesis account of creation has been steadily discredited by scientific theories about the origin of the cosmos and Darwin's evolutionary theory of the origin of species. By all except Christian fundamentalists, the biblical story of creation is now treated as poetry and myth.

Since the late eighteenth century theologians have tried to reconcile the growing body of scientific theory about the beginnings of the cosmos with a Christian understanding of God's role in creation. The Deists, for example, argued that God was a craftsman who assembled the universe as a giant mechanism that would operate according to scientific laws. This would mean that science is merely uncovering the mind and purposes of God. Process theologians (see separate entry) have argued that God is caught up in the evolutionary processes of creation. Others, such as Arthur Peacock, argue that science and religion offer different but complementary accounts of the same reality. In this way modern science and a theology of creation can both be right, even when they appear to be saying different things.

In the twentieth century, under the influence of phenomenology, some theologians have talked about the world – and indeed, God himself – as having the qualities of a 'gift'. But the givenness of the world does not point in some naïve way to a giver; rather, thinking of God and his creation as 'gift' helps us to think about what our response to this givenness should be. Interesting as this is, the theology of 'gift' dodges the scientific question of how exactly the world is 'given' to us.

The doctrine of creation remains one of the most hotly contested in Christian theology, not only because of the issue of science and religion, but also because many other theological arguments and ethical views depend upon how we think about God's creative action. In the heated Anglican discussions about sexuality, for example, those against homosexuality have argued that God created a world in which sex should take place only within the heterosexual pattern of Adam and Eve. Other theologians have argued that since God made everything 'good', this must include lesbians and gay men. The creation story is also at the centre of debates about the ethics of marriage and divorce.

THINKERS

St Augustine (354–430) argued strongly, against Gnostics such as the Manichaeans, that God was the sole creator and that he had made a good creation.

Thomas Aquinas (1225–74) followed Augustine in arguing that God created nothing evil, and that evil is the 'privation of good'. (See entry on Evil.)

Jean-Luc Marion (1946–) puts the concept of 'givenness' at the centre of his theology. When we analyse our existence down to its most basic (primordial) foundation, all we can say is that we live in a state of 'having been given'. This 'given' state is, Marion argues, not simple but a complex mixture of both presence and absence.

Pierre Teilhard de Chardin (1881–1955) argued that the Genesis story is a metaphor for God's creative action, rather than a literal account. He saw creation as a process unfolding towards an 'Omega Point', when the universe would have reached its final state.

IDEAS

Creation ordinances: the term used to refer to basic regulations which (according to the book of Genesis) were set down by God at the time of creation, such as keeping the Sabbath and the institution of marriage.

Creatio ex nihilo: the idea that God created the universe out of nothing.

Creatio continua: the idea that creation is a continual process.

Creationism: The fundamentalist belief that God literally created the world in six days.

Demiurge: a figure in some religions who is responsible for the creation of the physical universe.

Dominionism/dominion theology: a right-wing theology in the United States that supports ideas of Christian theocracy and the Christian entitlement to 'subdue' and 'dominate' the world. (See entry for Ecotheology.)

Imago Dei: the doctrine that humans are created in the image of God.

BOOKS

Jürgen Moltmann, *God in Creation: A New Theology of Creation and the Spirit of God* (Augsburg Fortress, 1993)

Arthur Peacock, *Creation and the World of Science: The Re-Shaping of Belief* (OUP, 2004)

The Death of God

The idea that God has disappeared both practically and theoretically from human life.

In one sense, the idea of the death of God is intensely biblical and orthodox. In the passion narratives we hear how God, in the form of Jesus, died on the cross. The body laid in the tomb is God's corpse. Orthodox theology has always insisted upon the indivisibility of God, which makes it difficult to argue that only Jesus died on the cross. The death of Jesus is the death of God – although, of course, the story continues to tell of God's resurrection.

The death of God on the cross is one of the most extraordinary and radical features of Christian theology. In the crucifixion, God apparently sacrifices his own life. But if God is eternal, how can he die? If God is unchanging, how can he change from 'living' to 'dead'? And if God is omniscient, would he not know about his resurrection in advance, thereby making his 'death' a charade? Here we see trinitarian doctrine collapsing, as it often does, into a tangle of paradoxes. As the hymn puts it:

> 'Tis mystery all!
> The Immortal dies –
> Who can explore his strange design?

The idea of 'the death of God' started to gain a new relevance when the nineteenth-century philosopher Hegel put the concept at the centre of his theology. He argued that the death of God was 'the negation of negation': a necessary and decisive step in the history of the world. Hegel believed that God had to die as an historical figure in order to become real as an eternal idea of perfect human society. The death of God as a human being opens up the age of God as Spirit. In other words, God's death permits him to become more universal: incarnate in the whole of human society and not merely in one individual.

The death of God reaches its best-known expression in the writings of Friedrich Nietzsche (*Thus Spoke Zarathustra* and *The Gay Science*). He tells the parable of the madman who proclaims in the town square that God is dead and that all our reference points have vanished. The townspeople say he is crazy and the madman departs, saying he has come before his time.

'The death of God' is Nietzsche's shorthand for the disappearance of all foundational ideas: truth, goodness, reality, beauty, progress, facts, and so on. Nietzsche's hero is the pre-Socratic philosopher Heraclitus, who argued that the world has no stable truths, but is in endless change. Nietzsche blames Plato and Christianity for covering up Heraclitus' wisdom with the illusion that the world is founded on theological realities. Slowly, since Plato, humanity has begun to glimpse that we create our own ideas of truth and that God is just another human invention. Nietzsche believed that a few people (called 'over-people') had the strength to face this truth, but that most of us would follow the herd and cling to our illusions.

Depending on who you speak to, Nietzsche is either a brilliant prophet who could foresee the anti-foundationalism which would be characteristic of modernity, or a philosopher who failed to acknowledge that all his own thinking depended upon 'a hidden theology' of foundational concepts. In recent years, for example, the Radical Orthodoxy school of theology has argued that the death of God is a humanist 'myth' that depends upon concealed metaphysical presuppositions – in particular, the existence of the self. Either way, for good or ill, Nietzsche is probably the most influential philosopher of modern times.

In the 1960s, some radical Christians argued that it is possible to have a version of Christianity that holds the death of God as a Christian truth. Drawing on Blake and Hegel, Thomas Altizer's *The Gospel of Christian Atheism* (1967) argued that God 'annihilated' himself on the cross in order to empty himself fully into the world. Few would go as far as Altizer, but most theologians now accept the death of God as a cultural phenomenon that theology must address.

THINKERS

Thomas Altizer (1927–) was the leading thinker in 'death of God theology'. He argued that theology cannot find its future 'unless it passes through and freely wills its own death and dissolution. Theology is now impelled to employ the very language that proclaims the "death of God"' (*Radical Theology and The Death of God*, p. 16).

Thomas Aquinas (1225–74) said that Christians 'recognize in the cross of Christ the death of God, by which he has conquered the devil and the world'.

Matthew Arnold (1822–88) spoke in his poem 'Dover Beach' (1867) of the 'melancholy, long, withdrawing roar' as the 'Sea of Faith' recedes.

Albert Camus (1913–60), the existentialist atheist, commented in *The Myth of Sisyphus*: 'To kill God is to become god oneself; it is to realize already on this earth the eternal life of which the Gospel speaks.'

Don Cupitt (1935–) argued in a ground-breaking book, *Taking Leave of God* (1980), that we need God as a guiding 'ideal' or 'the sum of our values', but that the idea of a 'real' God is redundant.

Ludwig Feuerbach (1804–72) argued that God is simply a projection of human concerns.

Eberhard Jüngel (1934–) argued in *God as the Mystery of the World* (1983) that the concept of the 'death of God' should be understood only to refer to Christ's death, and that this death is necessary.

Martin Luther (1483–1546) famously said in a chorale that *Gott selbst ist tot* ('God himself is dead') – a line that later influenced Hegel. It is amusing to think that Nietzsche probably sang this chorale as a child, and that Martin Luther may have inadvertently given Nietzsche the idea that God is dead.

Karl Marx (1818–83) argued that the concept of God was a tool of oppression, and that belief in God would disappear naturally as oppression was lifted.

Blaise Pascal (1623–62) proclaimed that 'the great God Pan is dead' – a reference to the loss of a sense of divinity in the world.

Praxeas (second century AD) was a modalist who argued that God the Father died on the cross with Christ. (See 'Modalism' in 'The Trinity'.)

Gabriel Vahanian (1927–) argued in *God is Dead: The culture of our post-Christian era* (1957) that, for modern people, atheism is a way of life.

Max Weber (1864–1920) coined the phrase 'the disenchantment of the world' to describe the way in which secular thinking has dissolved the mystery of the cosmos.

IDEAS

Patripassianism: the belief that God the Father died on the cross with Christ.

Anti-Foundationalism: the belief that our thoughts and perceptions are not grounded in facts, truths and realities.

Kenosis: the idea that God 'emptied himself' in order to become human.

BOOKS

Thomas Altizer, *The Gospel of Christian Atheism* (Westminster Press, 1966)

Jackson L. Ice and John J. Carey (eds.), *The Death of God Debate* (Westminster Press, 1967)

Thomas W. Ogletree, *The Death of God Controversy* (Abingdon Press, 1966)

The Divine Attributes

The analysis of God by considering his various qualities.

One way of approaching theology is to analyse God's various attributes. Many of these attributes are given in the Bible – such as God being holy and all loving – but others, such as God's simplicity, derive from philosophical ideas (mostly neo-Platonic) about the necessary character of God. There is a basic underlying tension here between the Hebraic story of God found in the Bible and the Greek philosophical conception of divinity.

Producing a simple list of potential divine attributes is fairly unproblematic, since God, by definition, has every attribute in perfection. So when we consider God's power, we must conclude that he is omnipotent (all powerful), and when we consider his knowledge, we must say that he is omniscient (all knowing). Other doctrines affirm God's immutability (unchangeability), eternity (timelessness), impassibility (freedom from passions), aseity (self-sufficiency) and simplicity (indivisibility).

But difficulties soon present themselves. A first set of problems arises when we try to reconcile the various attributes. So if God is simple, is this not a restriction on his omnipotent capacity to be as complicated or as simple as he likes? And if God is unchangeable, how is it possible for him to exercise his power at any moment in time, since the exercise of his power would involve him in a process of change? Theologians – particularly scholastic theologians – have offered intricate answers to these kinds of questions, but they become increasingly convoluted and unconvincing.

A radical alternative to harmonising the attributes is to accept that God may be paradoxical. Søren Kierkegaard argued in *Philosophical Fragments* (1844) that the doctrine of the two natures of Christ – divine and human – is an absolute paradox. Rowan

Williams has offered another rationale for theological paradoxes: 'We utter paradoxes not to mystify or avoid problems, but precisely to stop ourselves making things easy by pretending that some awkward or odd feature of our perception isn't really there. We speak in paradoxes because we have to speak in a way that keeps a question alive' (*Open to Judgement*).

Another set of problems arises when we consider the logical contradictions arising from the absolute nature of the attributes. If we were to say that God is very powerful, the problem would not arise, but we make his power an *absolute omnipotence*. If God's power is absolute, is it possible for him to create a rock that is too heavy for himself to lift? The answer, logically, must be both yes and no. Another version of this paradox runs: 'It is the final proof of God's omnipotence that he need not exist in order to save us.'

A further area of difficulty concerns the very act of dividing God into separate qualities and faculties. This reduces God to a list of human categories and contradicts the doctrine of divine simplicity, which says that God is not composed of parts.

The main theological objection to the analysis of divine attributes is that the process appears to limit God to human ideas about the *necessary* nature of God. Nicholas of Cusa suggested an alternative approach: the consideration of the *possible* nature of God or, as he called it, God's possible-actuality (*possest*). He argued that God's infinite possibility can contain 'the coincidence of opposites'. In this way God embraces his own paradoxes.

THINKERS

Thomas Aquinas (1224–74) argued in his *Summa Theologiae* that God's perfection means that his attributes are necessarily unified. The attributes appear to be diverse because of the limitations of human thought.

St Augustine (354–430) stressed the unity of the attributes, but also relished the possibilities for divine paradox: 'What art Thou then, my God? Most highest, most good, most potent, most omnipotent; most merciful and most just; most hidden and most present; most beautiful and most strong, standing firm and elusive, unchangeable and all-changing; never new, never old; ever working, ever at rest' (*Confessions*).

D. M. Baillie (1887–1954) argued (in *God was in Christ*) against the doctrine that God is impassible (impervious to suffering) on the grounds that impassibility could not accommodate Christ's agony on the cross.

Dante Alighieri (1265–1321) describes (in *The Divine Comedy*) God's three primary attributes, corresponding to the persons of the Holy Trinity: Power, Wisdom, Love.

Colin Gunton (1941–2003) argues (in *Act and Being*) that the divine attributes can only be understood within a narrative about what God does: 'God is what he does and does what he is.'

Gilbert de la Porrée (1070–1154) argued that there was a basic distinction between the essential nature of God and his attributes. His views were deemed heretical by the Catholic Church.

Albrecht Ritschl (1822–89) argued that God's nature was love and that all other attributes must derive from this.

IDEAS

Coincidentia oppositorum: or coincidence of opposites, a view developed by Nicholas of Cusa in the fifteenth century (in *On Learned Ignorance*) and recently revived by Thomas Altizer, that sees all contradictions contained within God's infinity.

Divine command theory: this states that God is not subject to our definition of goodness and determines what is good through his ordinances.

The Euthrypo dilemma was posed by Socrates in Plato's *Euthrypo* and asks whether 'God' and 'goodness' are one and the same. Is an action good because God approves of it? Or does God approve of good actions because they are good? The latter position would put goodness above God.

The problem of the one and the many: the ancient philosophical puzzle of how to reconcile the diversity of the world with its unity.

BOOKS

Colin Gunton, *Act and Being: Towards a Theology of the Divine Attributes* (Eerdmans, 2002)

Joshua Hoffman and Gary Rosenkrantz, *The Divine Attributes* (Blackwell, 2002)

Doctrine

The agreed or authorised teachings of a church.

In the course of history, all sorts of theological ideas are suggested and discussed, but not all these ideas attain the status of doctrines. Doctrines are those theological beliefs that form the official teaching of a church (the word 'doctrine' literally means 'teaching'). Doctrines express orthodox belief and may take the form of creeds, confessions, statements and catechisms.

The very notion that the Church should codify its teaching in doctrines is problematic. Jesus offers his teaching mostly in the form of stories and does not seem very interested in definitive statements of belief. Furthermore, Jesus' message concerns a way of living, loving and forgiving that feels out of keeping with dogmatic teaching. Tolstoy, for example, argued that it was 'ridiculous' to fix the Christian message in abstract doctrines, when Christianity is really a way of living life in relationship with God.

Yet churches have inevitably been obliged to develop doctrines to define their identities. Even apparently non-doctrinal denominations (such as the Quakers) have practices and structures that reflect implicit doctrines. Indeed, the idea of a church without any doctrines whatsoever is unimaginable.

But the process of turning the mostly narrative texts of the Bible into doctrines has been a fraught business. St Paul complained of schisms in the church in Corinth, and disputes over what the Church should be teaching have continued ever since. Arguments over the major doctrines of the Christian faith – such as the Trinity and the nature of Christ – were not 'settled' until the fourth and fifth centuries. There are, at a conservative estimate, 35,000 Christian denominations world-wide, each claiming to have the truest doctrines.

To insiders, denominational divisions are clearly of great importance. But from the outside, the differences between the denominations can appear petty and technical. Consequently, doctrinal disputes often bring the churches into public disrepute, because outsiders simply cannot understand why the issues matter.

The traditional conception of doctrine is what could be called the 'propositional' view that doctrines are absolute theological pronouncements from which there can be no deviation. This makes all discussion of doctrine a win–lose contest where only one party can be right, since it follows from the 'rightness' of one party that the other must necessarily be wrong. There is no possibility of more than one correct view of the truth, and once fixed, the doctrine must be defended for all time. This is why the Roman Catholic Church waited until 1992 to change the doctrinal position that it had taken in 1633 on Galileo's astronomical theories.

In practice, of course, doctrines have changed over time, with new doctrines being added to the body of teaching, and with others being amended (see 'Atonement').

In recent decades theologians have been re-thinking the status of doctrine, particularly in the light of twentieth-century developments in the philosophy of language. Wittgenstein, in particular, argued that language does not merely describe the world or express our ideas: all language is embedded in a 'form of life' and cannot be understood apart from the cultural milieu in which it is used. Taking up Wittgenstein's ideas, George Lindbeck (*The Nature of Doctrine*, 1984) has proposed that orthodoxy is expressed in the complete life of the Church and not simply in its doctrinal formulae. Doctrines operate like rules that help us to define and organise the 'form of life' of any particular church.

John Milbank (*Theology and Social Theory*, 1990) has gone beyond Lindbeck to suggest that doctrine cannot be abstracted into rules but is the complete mythos or lived-narrative reality of the Christian faith: both the story of Jesus and the ongoing history of the Church. The principal weakness of Milbank's approach is that the Christian *mythos* comes in more than 35,000 versions, and he provides no criteria for determining which is most true. Indeed, if Milbank were to provide criteria, he would have to concede that Lindbeck is correct in insisting on doctrinal 'rules'.

A more satisfactory modern understanding of doctrine has been offered by David Tracy (*The Analogical Imagination*, 1982; *Plurality and Ambiguity*, 1987), who accepts that there will be many valid versions of Christianity and argues that doctrine is constituted by the conversation about what he calls 'the religious classic'. Tracy uses the word 'classic' to mean a religion's governing text, idea, ritual, event or person. In the case of Christianity, the 'classic' is the story of Jesus.

When we look at the debates and controversies that have made up, and continue to make up, the history of doctrine, Tracy's view has a ring of truth about it. Christian doctrines aren't handed down from the heavens but are the result of conversations and arguments about what constitutes the true faith.

THINKERS

Hans Frei (1922–88) inspired the New Yale School of Theology by thinking of doctrine in narrative terms (*Theology and Narrative*, 1993).

Adolf von Harnack (1851–1930) was a powerful liberal critic of dogmatic Christianity. He argued that the earliest Christians were concerned with a way of life, and that doctrinal belief was the result of Greek influence in Christian theology: 'in its conception and construction [doctrine] is a product of the Greek spirit on the soil of the Gospel' (*The History of Dogma*).

Vincent of Lérins (?–?450) described the ideal of true doctrine as 'what has been believed everywhere, always, and by all' (*Commonitorium* II.3). In reality, of course, this ideal has never been realised.

Bernard Lonergan (1904–84) saw doctrine as a process of evolution and exploration in understanding divine mystery, arguing that the process of human understanding was not merely cerebral, but involved the full range of human experience.

John Henry Newman (1801–90) argued in his *Essay on the Development of Christian Doctrine* (1845) that inconsistencies in the teaching of the Church could be explained by taking an evolutionary view of the history of doctrine: 'The highest and most wonderful truths, though communicated to the world once for all by inspired teachers ... have required ... longer time and deeper thought for their full elucidation.'

Karl Rahner (1904–84) argued that Christian doctrine must be rooted in our common experience of being human: 'no doctrine of God is possible any more without a doctrine of man, no theology without anthropology.'

Ian Ramsey (1915–72) argued in *Religious Language* that the basis of doctrine lies in 'disclosure' situations.

Leo Tolstoy (1879–1910) complained that 'religious doctrine is professed in some other realm … disconnected from life' (A *Confession*, ch. 1).

Ernst Troeltsch (1865–1923) argued that the message of Jesus was ethical rather than doctrinal: 'We are no longer in the business of fixing permanent dogmas from an inspired Bible. Instead, we formulate teachings which express the essence of Christian piety.'

IDEAS

The Assumption of the Blessed Virgin Mary: a 'new' doctrine, controversially adopted by the Roman Catholic Church in 1950, that the Blessed Virgin Mary was taken, body and soul, straight up to heaven after her death.

Catechesis: the teaching of the Church in its practical form.

Didache (pronounced 'did-ee-kay'): the Greek term for 'teaching'.

Dogma: the absolute teachings of a religion. Some theologians prefer to differentiate doctrine (the expression of theological truth) from dogma (the making of absolutist claims).

Heterodoxy: beliefs and arguments that are at variance from the Church's official teaching.

The Magisterium: the official body in Roman Catholicism that decides the true teaching of the Church.

Orthodoxy: the official version of Christianity.

Scepticism: the tendency to doubt all dogmatic claims.

BOOKS

George Pattison, *A Short Course in Christian Doctrine* (SCM, 2005)

Colin Gunton (ed.), *The Cambridge Companion to Christian Doctrine* (CUP, 1997)

Ecotheology

Theology that affirms the primacy and importance of the natural cosmos.

In the past 30 years or so, the traditional doctrine of creation has faced a fundamental challenge from ecological theologians who argue that the Christian creation myth supports the supremacy of humanity over creation, rather than the mutual interdependence of humanity and nature. The idea, set out in the book of Genesis, that we have 'dominion' over nature and are entitled to do what we like to the world, has allegedly given theological justification to our abuse of nature and its resources:

> We shall continue to have a worsening ecological crisis until we reject the Christian axiom that nature has no reason for existence save to serve man ... Both our present science and our present technology are so tinctured with orthodox Christian arrogance toward nature that no solution for our ecological crisis can be expected from them alone. Since the roots of our trouble are so largely religious, the remedy must also be essentially religious, whether we call it that or not.
>
> (Lynn White, 'On the Historical Roots of our Ecological Crisis', in Roger Gottlieb (ed.), *This Sacred Earth*, Routledge, 2003)

The human abuse of nature has become ever more obvious as our industries and technologies have started to impact on the natural environment. Global warming is an obvious example, but there are plenty of others: bio-technology, intensive farming, deforestation, the exploitation of finite natural resources, and pollution. As the negative, even catastrophic, effects of our abuse of nature become clear, so theologians have begun to question the theological premise that nature is ours to use as we wish. The traditionally anthropocentric view of creation has been unsettled, and it is now suggested that humans should be regarded as just another part of nature, rather than nature's crowning glory.

So-called 'ecotheology' offers an understanding of creation as a cosmic system which incorporates humanity. Human beings do not have rights of dominion over nature, but are within nature, and must look to nature to understand what it means to be human. This implies a revision of the traditional view of God, which has emphasised God's power over the natural world, rather than his nurturing creativity within the cosmos.

Unlike some academic theology, ecotheology has direct implications both for individual conduct and for policy at every level of government, from the local council to the United Nations. It may be possible to study narrative theology, for example, and leave one's personal and political life unchallenged, but ecotheology concerns our global human livelihood and cannot be a merely theoretical pursuit.

THINKERS

St Augustine (354–430) argued strongly against Gnostics, such as the Manicheans, that God was the sole creator and that he had made a good creation.

Sallie McFague (1933–) argues that we need to coin new 'immanental' metaphors for God which do not portray him as a monarch, dominating and controlling nature.

Lynn White (1907–87) published a seminal article in 1967, 'The Historical Roots of our Ecological Crisis'. White argued that our modern ecological difficulties originate in Christian ideas about humanity's relationship with nature.

IDEAS

Cosmic Christianity: a term used by Mircea Eliade to describe forms of agrarian Christianity which emphasise the human relationship with the cosmos, the cycle of the seasons and the use of symbols drawn from the natural world.

Creation ordinances: a term which refers to the basic regulations set down by God at the time of creation, such as keeping the Sabbath and the institution of marriage.

Dominionism/dominion theology: a right-wing theology in the United States that supports ideas of Christian theocracy and the Christian entitlement to 'subdue' and 'dominate' the world.

Specieism: a term used by Peter Singer in his book, *Animal Liberation, A New Ethic for Our Treatment of Animals* (1975). Specieism refers to the exploitation of other animal species by human beings.

BOOKS

Sallie McFague, *The Body of God: An Ecological Theology* (SCM Press, 1993)

H. Paul Santmire, *The Travail of Nature: The Ambiguous Ecological Promise of Christian Theology* (Augsburg Fortress Press, 1985)

David G. Hallman (ed.), *Ecotheology: Voices from South and North* (Orbis Books, 1996)

Matthew Fox, *A New Reformation: Creation Spirituality and the Transformation of Christianity* (Inner Traditions, 2006)

Eschatology

Traditionally, the rather depressing study of 'the four last things': death, judgement, heaven and hell. Now theologians use the term 'eschatology' more optimistically to mean the study of human destiny.

Christianity is a future-orientated religion, and the enticement of heaven and the threat of hell have always been fundamental to its theology. So the study of the 'end times' has an important place in Christian thinking. This subject has been called 'eschatology'. Like many theological concepts, the term derives from a Greek word – *eschatos*, meaning 'last'.

The idea that our final destiny shapes our present reality (also called 'teleology') has its roots in the philosophy of Aristotle, who argued that 'nature does nothing in vain' but is always working towards final ends: the egg is working towards becoming a chicken, the seed is working to become a plant.

The eschatology of the Old Testament is most clearly evident in the Prophets, who spoke, in the words of Isaiah, about a time when 'the Lord will be your everlasting light, and your days of mourning shall be ended. Your people shall all be righteous; they shall possess the land for ever' (Isa. 60:20–21). By and large, the prophets spoke optimistically about the fulfilment of history.

By the second century BC, the popularity of prophetic teaching had waned. New 'apocalyptic' writers (such as Daniel) took to the stage, teaching that the 'end times' would involve the violent closure of human history, and the opening of a new era of divine rule. The eschatology of Jesus, St Paul and the early Church was also predominantly apocalyptic, with visions of cosmic disaster, final judgement, mysterious creatures and the founding of a perfect society under divine governance.

Throughout Christian history, there have been Chiliastic movements preaching about the end of the world. This view is not held by the mainstream churches, but in the USA, the idea of 'the Rapture', when God will take to himself all the saved, is extremely popular.

Eschatology shifted gear in the early nineteenth century when philosophers and theologians – notably Herder and Hegel (and Vico, a generation before them) – started to think more deeply about the shape and purpose of human history. Herder noted that history appeared to fall into phases and epochs, and that human cultures were very different at different times. Hegel believed that the phases of human history were all heading logically towards a perfect state.

Many modern theologians latched on to this idea and argued that Christians had a basic responsibility to change the world. Christian socialists such as Fredrick Dennison Maurice and Stewart Headlam argued that God's kingdom on earth would replace the divisions, injustice and cruelty of society.

In the twentieth century such utopian dreams, and the confidence that human beings really could improve themselves, were crushed by a long series of hideous human failures: including two world wars, the Holocaust, BSE, AIDS and the genocide in Rwanda.

Only a fool could now believe that human beings can make a perfect world. So where is the perfect future going to come from? Modern eschatology has now generally lost its nerve, and talks vaguely about 'hope' rather than any real expectation that we will ever see the kingdom of God on earth.

THINKERS

G. W. F. Hegel (1770–1831) believed that history was divided up into three phases: the Age of the Father, the Age of the Son, and the Age of the Spirit. The destiny of humanity was to reach the Age of the Spirit, when human affairs would perfectly conform to the mind of God. Hegel believed that this 'end of history' had been achieved in nineteenth-century Prussia!

Karl Jaspers (1883–1969) argued that life is affected by a horizon of events called 'limit situations': death, suffering, guilt, conflict. These situations 'illuminate' our existence and, in turn, we are able to read the signs of divine transcendence. History evolves as a series of 'Axial' phases in which human knowledge and self-awareness develop. Jaspers believed we are awaiting a third Axial age in which human beings will become fully aware both of their existence and of God.

Jürgen Moltmann (1926–) argues that eschatology must take the form of a theology of hope. We can have hope because the history of the world is an ongoing revelation of God's promises of an ideal future. The Bible is 'the history book of God's promises' (*The Theology of Hope*).

Wolfhart Pannenberg (1928–) argues that eschatology is crucial to an authentic Christianity. God determines the present through the future, by setting before us the vision of the kingdom of God. This kingdom is both something we work for and a future reality which shapes present history. The resurrection is a sign of the coming kingdom. Indeed, God himself is a God of the Future, fashioning the train of historical events behind him. A major weakness in Pannenberg's eschatology is that he never explains properly *how* the future can determine the present.

Albert Schweitzer (1875–1965) argued that Jesus was an eschatological prophet who came to warn of the imminent end of the world.

IDEAS

The apocalypse: a Greek word meaning 'unveiling', 'apocalypse' refers to the end of the world.

Chiliasm: the belief that God will bring the world to an end.

Dialectics: the idea that history evolves through the conflict of opposites.

Heilsgeschichte: a German term meaning 'salvation history' – the story of humanity from its fall in the Garden of Eden to its salvation in the Kingdom of Heaven.

Parousia: a Greek word for the second coming of Christ.

Prolepsis: a Greek word meaning the 'anticipation' of the end times.

Providence: the belief that God provides for our needs as history unfolds.

Realised eschatology: the belief that the final destiny of the world will be achieved within human history.

The second coming: the return of Christ at the time of the apocalypse.

Soteriology: the study of salvation.

Teleology: the idea that the end determines the means.

BOOKS

Paul Fiddes, *The Promised End: Eschatology in Theology and Literature* (Blackwell, 2000)

Jürgen Moltmann, *The Theology of Hope* (SCM, 2002)

Evil

The fact of suffering in the world begs the question of whether something called 'evil' exists, and why an all-loving and all-powerful God appears to tolerate its existence.

Any examination of human life reveals the existence of extreme cruelty and suffering, which we call 'evil'. Some suffering appears to be directly connected with our well-being, such as the pain that deters us from touching fire. And other forms of suffering appear to be 'necessary' for our survival as a species, such as the labour pains that precede birth. But other kinds of suffering appear to be random: in the same hospital one happy couple can be celebrating the birth of their healthy child, while another is grieving the death of their sick infant. Whether we are religious or not, it is very natural to ask whether the tragedy of the world means anything. Is there perhaps some 'evil force' at work in the world? And if so, how could a God permit this force to exist? Western, Christian thinking has thrown up five classic responses:

1. *The Tragic Response.* The reality of suffering could lead us to reject the existence of any good God, or indeed, any real goodness in the

world. As it says on the T-shirt: 'Life is shit and then you die.' This is a very bleak response to suffering, but also a very real one that most theologians ignore. Christian theologians tend to assume that we must reach a Christian solution to the problem of evil. The truth is that the fact of evil quite often leads to the conclusion that there is no God and that we are on our own in a dangerous and meaningless universe.

2. *The Trusting Response.* The opposite response would be to make a complete act of trust in God's benevolent, divine rule over human affairs. Childhood leukaemia may look tragic to us, but from God's superior perspective, even the most hideous suffering could be serving a good purpose. If God is a good God, and we believe this utterly, then we should not question him, but rather accept life, praising and thanking him for every event. 'The Lord gives and the Lord takes away: Blessed be the name of the Lord' (Job 1:21).

3. *The Dualistic Response.* The presence of both goodness and suffering in the world could suggest that the world is governed by a Star Wars-type battle between good and evil forces: God and Satan, for example. The Gnostics tried to explain evil by positing the existence of a corrupt God, but orthodox Christianity has generally rejected such dualisms.

Having said that, traditional Christianity has been rather confused about dualism, because it has also argued for the reality of the devil. Unless we argue that the devil is mysteriously doing God's work (and some theology comes close to saying this), then the existence of the devil would require a theory of theological and moral dualism.

4. *The Non-existence-of-Evil Response.* This response derives from Platonic philosophy and argues that 'evil' is not a positive reality but the absence of good. The argument starts by equating reality with 'goodness' or 'God'. If we accept that the only 'real' things in the world are the good things made by God, then evil cannot logically exist. This means that evil is only apparent. A paralysed person does not possess a positive reality called 'paralysis' but suffers from the absence of movement. Thus evil is defined negatively as that which is 'not good' or 'not God'. Both Augustine and Aquinas argued in this way that evil was unreal. Whatever the logical attractions of this approach, we must surely doubt whether it is

really satisfactory to say, for example, that the Holocaust was only the absence of good.

5. *The Moral Response.* A final argument sees life as a kind of 'school of morals' in which we humans have to suffer in order to learn. God wants us to be truly free, so he gives us the freedom even to do evil. The suffering of others gives us opportunities for compassion, and our own suffering gives us the opportunity to show dignity in the face of tragedy. While it is true that we can learn from suffering, the Moral Response paints a bizarre picture of God as a vicious schoolmaster devising mind-boggling (but educational) forms of pain for his students. It would be hard to worship such a deity, who seems incompatible with the Christian image of a God of Love.

These five responses are all 'religious' reactions to evil. So it could be argued that evil is only a problem if we start out with a belief in God. An atheist could say that suffering is simply a fact that must be dealt with practically (or not dealt with at all), but that suffering does not imply the existence of 'evil'. This view, if correct, would make evil a pseudo-problem, artificially created by religious people.

This 'secular' view is in fact a cold-blooded version of the Tragic Response. The problem of evil can be expressed in secular form as the question of why suffering exists at all, and how we should respond to it. The secularist may balk at the word 'evil', but would presumably accept some other general classification of pain and suffering. Even without positing the existence of God, the question of the purpose of suffering still stands, even if only to be dismissed with the response that suffering has no purpose. In responding thus, of course, the secularist has provided an answer to the problem of evil.

THINKERS

St Augustine (354–430) offers what is probably the most famous analysis of evil in his *Confessions*, which conclude that evil does not exist. (See 'The *Privatio Boni* Argument' below.)

René Descartes (1596–1650) posed the possibility that God was in fact an evil demon replacing the real world with a dream of reality. Descartes quickly rejected this possibility, saying that it would be contradictory for God to do anything so sneaky.

Fyodor Dostoyevsky (1821–81) tells the story of Jesus and 'The

Grand Inquisitor' (in *The Brothers Karamazov*), which reflects upon the paradoxes of human freedom and suffering. The Grand Inquisitor blames Jesus for giving us freedom and so sowing the seeds of the destruction of his own kingdom.

Georg Hegel (1770–1831) argued that 'the negative aspects of existence' can only make sense once we have understood 'the ultimate design of the world' (*Lectures on the Philosophy of World History*).

Gottfried Leibniz (1646–1716) argued in *The Theodicy* (1710) that God created not a perfect world, but 'the best of all possible worlds'.

Justin Martyr (c. 100–185) argued that God made the world from pre-existing matter and that this accounts for the presence of evil (the unorthodox 'Gnostic' view).

Friedrich Nietzsche (1844–1900) argued that 'good' and 'evil' are imagined categories that do not really exist. Instead, the world is a play of forces which has no moral meaning. Good and bad events do not 'mean' anything, and we should accept life as it comes. This acceptance of life is the secret of true human happiness.

Jean-Jacques Rousseau (1712–78) took the view that humanity had corrupted God's perfect creation: 'Everything is good as it leaves the hands of the Author of Nature; everything degenerates in the hands of men' (*Émile*).

Alexander Pope (1688–1744), in his *Essay on Man*, argued that we cannot understand the mind of God and should concentrate on understanding and improving the human world: 'Know then thyself, presume not God to scan,/ the proper study of mankind is man.'

Elie Wiesel (1928–): a Jewish thinker whose play *The Trial of God* brings God to account for his alleged cruelty and indifference to the suffering of his people.

IDEAS

Manichaeism: an early Gnostic heresy (famously refuted by Augustine in his *Confessions*) which ascribed evil to the existence of a lesser god of matter.

Moral evil is the suffering produced by human actions. It can be blamed on humanity, although this begs the question asked by St

Augustine: Who planted this seed of evil intention within us?

Natural evil is the suffering produced within nature itself.

Natural disasters often provoke public debate about the existence of evil. The Lisbon Earthquake of 1755 killed several thousand people and sparked responses from philosophers all over Europe: Kant, Voltaire, Rousseau and Goethe. In the Aberfan Disaster of 1966, 116 children were killed when a mud-slide smothered their school shortly after morning prayers. The tragedy prompted national reflections on the existence of God. The Tsunami Disaster of 2004 killed 250,000, causing people world-wide to ask about the meaning of natural evil.

The *Privatio Boni* Argument (literally 'privation of good') says that evil is just the absence of good.

Process Theology argues that God is still in the process of forming a perfect creation and that evil is slowly being worked out of existence. (See pp. 106–9)

Theodicy is the attempt 'to justify the ways of God to man'.

BOOKS

Susan Neiman, *Evil in Modern Thought* (Princeton University Press, 2002)

John Hick, *Evil and the God of Love* (Palgrave Macmillan, 1985)

Faith

Faith is a form of trust that does not depend upon knowledge of the object in which one has faith.

The word 'faith' is used loosely to mean adherence to a particular religious tradition. So we speak, for example, of 'the Catholic faith' or 'the Jewish faith'. The *faculty* of faith, however, is an act of trust which is not dependent upon knowledge or experience. We say colloquially that 'faith is blind', meaning that faith can operate when there may be no evidence to support an act of faith, or even when the evidence appears to contradict our faith. As it is put in the letter to the Hebrews: 'Faith is the assurance of things hoped for, the conviction of things not seen' (Heb. 11:1).

The Roman Catholic Church has always insisted that true faith must be faith in the doctrines of the Church. For a faith to be true, it is argued, the object of faith must also be true. A faith in the man in the moon, however devoutly held, would be a false faith. The Church has the God-given authority to direct believers to the things in which they ought to place their trust. So, runs the argument, faith in the Church's teachings is the only credible faith that we can trust with absolute confidence.

The trouble with this argument is that it replaces faith with knowledge. If the truth of our faith has been revealed in advance to the Church, then real faith is no longer required, because the truth of our beliefs is not in doubt. The individual believer merely has to agree that the Church knows best.

Martin Luther offered an alternative Protestant view, emphasising faith as a direct relationship between the individual believer and God, which does not require the mediation of the Church. Faith happens only by God's grace, Luther argued, so is completely outside human control, knowledge or reasoning: 'Reason must be deluded, blinded, and destroyed. Faith must trample underfoot all reason, sense, and understanding.'

Søren Kierkegaard took the Protestant view to its extreme, arguing that true faith must be focused on an absurd or impossible goal. He extolled the higher religious virtue of 'the Knight of Faith'. The Knight is prepared to make 'a teleological suspension of the ethical' – meaning that she or he is prepared to obey the religious requirement of faith even if it appears to break ethical rules. This is 'faith by virtue of the absurd' and cannot be justified by reason or be reduced to knowledge. Abraham, whose faith in God was so unswerving that he was prepared to sacrifice his own son, is Kierkegaard's epitome of a Knight of Faith.

To rationalists such as the Deists and the Positivists, the exercise of reason and the quest for empirical knowledge were everything, and faith was considered unimportant or even dangerous. As Richard Dawkins has put it: 'Faith, being belief that isn't based on evidence, is the principal vice of any religion' (from 'Is Science a Religion?'). A number of critics have responded that even science presupposes a world-view for which there is no empirical evidence. Edmund Husserl, for example, argued that empiricism presumes the existence of a 'self' capable of making objective observations. In recent decades there has been a powerful popular reaction against empirical rationalism and a resurgence in faiths of various kinds, from New Age religions to Christian fundamentalism.

Recently, some more radical theologians (e.g. John Caputo and Gianni Vattimo), inspired by Jacques Derrida and other Continental philosophers, have been discussing the possibility of a faith without God, or a faith in a God who is absent. (See 'Negative Theology'.) This would be an ultimate and pure faith, operating without even the presupposition of the existence of God.

THINKERS

Albert Einstein (1879–1955) saw a role for faith in science: 'Scientists were rated as great heretics by the church, but they were truly religious men because of their faith in the orderliness of the universe.'

Adolf Harnack (1851–1930) argued that the first 'Jewish Christians' had a simple faith in Jesus which was turned by the Church into rigid dogma: 'How and by what influence was the living faith transformed into the creed to be believed, the surrender to Christ into a philosophic Christology?' (*History of Dogma*).

Immanuel Kant (1724–1804) argued that we must 'deny knowledge to make room for faith', meaning that our 'knowledge' about God is inadequate, so we can only grasp God in an act of faith. The implications of this are radical and far reaching, as Kant himself spelled out: 'Religion is conscientiousness. The holiness of the acceptance and the truthfulness of what man must confess to himself ... To have religion, the concept of God is not required (still less the postulate: "There is a God")' (*Opus Postumum*).

Martin Luther (1483–1546) regarded faith as the most important religious faculty: 'Faith is a living, bold trust in God's grace, so certain of God's favor that it would risk death a thousand times trusting in it' (*An Introduction to St Paul's Letter to the Romans*).

Baruch Spinoza (1632–77) declared that religious faith 'consists in honesty and sincerity of heart rather than in outward actions' (*Tractatus*).

IDEAS

Analogia fidei (from the Latin for 'analogy of faith'): the argument, associated with Karl Barth, that we cannot understand God's workings using human faculties, but only through God's action of revealing himself to us.

Belief: an opinion based upon evidence.

Creed: a formal statement of faith or beliefs.

Fideism: the view that religion only consists of acts of faith, because there can be no knowledge of theological objects.

Fides fiducialis: Martin Luther's doctrine of 'faith as trust'.

Justification by faith: the doctrine, championed by St Paul, St Augustine and Martin Luther, that 'the just shall live by faith' (Rom. 1:17).

The leap of faith: the act of believing, despite the lack of adequate evidence to support that belief.

Knowledge: beliefs that are true.

Sola fides: Martin Luther's principle that 'faith alone' justifies humanity to God.

BOOKS

Jaroslav Pelikan, *Credo: Historical and Theological Guide to Creeds and Confessions of Faith in the Christian Tradition* (Yale University Press, 2005)

Lesslie Newbigin, *Proper Confidence: Faith, Doubt, and Certainty in Christian Discipleship* (Eerdmans,1995)

Peter L. Berger, *Questions of Faith: A Skeptical Affirmation of Christianity* (Blackwell, 2003)

Feminist Theology

An approach to theology that aims to give women their true value.

Feminist theology began as a critical analysis of the neglect of women's experiences in Christian thinking and practice. Not only was traditional theology written by men with little regard for the distinctive voices of women, but much Christian theology was hatefully misogynistic. Tertullian's remark that women were 'the devil's gateway' was an extreme expression of an active misogyny at the heart of Christian theology.

Like feminism in general, feminist theology is not so much a distinct theory as a range of approaches and perspectives united by what one writer has called 'an ethical commitment to giving women their true value' (E. Wilson: *Hidden Agendas,* Tavistock, 1986). This commitment has found a range of expressions, from rights-based campaigns for equality, to radical 'goddess' theology, post-Christian feminism and lesbian feminism.

Although there were some earlier examples of feminist theology, such as Elizabeth Cady Stanton's *The Woman's Bible* (1895), it really took root in the late 1960s and early 1970s with the publication of landmark books by Mary Daly (*The Church and the Second Sex,* 1968) and Kari Borresen (*Subordination and Equivalence,* 1968).

Inspired by secular feminism, feminist theologians started treating the Christian tradition with active suspicion. Church structures were criticised for the exclusion and oppression of women, theological language was scrutinised for sexism and patriarchy, and the very structures of theological reasoning, including the male conception of God, were subjected to feminist critique.

At the centre of these approaches was a re-reading of the Christian tradition – in particular, the Bible. For example, Elisabeth Schüssler Fiorenza's *In Memory of Her: A Feminist Theological Reconstruction of Christian Origins* (1983) tried to look through the layers of patriarchal (mis)interpretation to detect the voices of women within the Christian Scriptures. Fiorenza showed how the production, translation and interpretation of the biblical texts operated to oppress women: 'A feminist reconstruction of history can no longer take patriarchal texts at face value but must critically interpret them in a feminist perspective.'

Although the critique of patriarchy was, and remains, very necessary, it has also been important for feminist theologians to present a constructive religious vision. For example, feminist critique exposed spirit–matter dualism as essentially sexist: the spirit was associated with the 'rational' male and matter with the 'feminine' body. This critique has been crucial to the development of numerous theologies of the body, sexuality, biology, bio-ethics and ecology.

One of the central issues has been the extent to which the traditions of the churches really provide adequate resources for a properly feminist theology. For some, like Sarah Coakley (*Powers and Submissions: Spirituality, Philosophy and Gender*, 2002), traditional trinitarian doctrine provides all the materials necessary for a feminist theology. But for others, the tradition must be radically adapted or supplemented with images of a feminine God, Christa (a feminine Christ), the figure of the Earth-goddess, or even the re-appropriation of witchcraft.

As with secular feminism, feminist theology has tended in the last decade to become ever more abstract and academic – and as a result, more distant from the practical campaigns for women's justice and social reform that characterised so-called 'First Wave' and 'Second Wave' feminism. The future of feminist theology lies perhaps not only in new theoretical developments but also in a reconnection with practical issues of justice for women.

THINKERS

Mary Daly (1928–): a radical feminist theologian who famously refused to admit male students to her classes at Boston College. In *Beyond God the Father* and subsequent works she argued that 'if God is male, then male is God. The divine patriarch castrates women as long as he is allowed to live on in the human imagination.' Daly used language and concepts in imaginative ways in order to disrupt patriarchy, which she believed was written into all our patterns of Western thought. She argued that we need to recover earlier concepts of God, particularly 'negative theology', Aquinas' theology of Being and his conception of 'God as a verb'.

Elisabeth Schüssler Fiorenza (1938–): a pioneer of feminist interpretation of the Bible.

Daphne Hampson (1944–) has argued in *Theology and Feminism* that feminism must follow a post-Christian trajectory because the Christian tradition, centred on a male Messiah, simply cannot be redeemed. Hampson says she has 'rejected the Christian myth … The myth is not neutral; it is highly dangerous. It is a brilliant, subtle, elaborate, male cultural projection.'

Carter Heyward (1945–): a lesbian feminist and one of the 11

Episcopal women 'illegally' ordained in Philadelphia in 1974. Heyward has drawn on Martin Buber's theology to develop a theology of 'right relation': 'We are born in relation, we live in relation, we die in relation' to one another, to the cosmos and to God.

John Knox (1505–72): a Reformation theologian and the author of a virulently misogynistic text entitled *The First Blast of the Trumpet Against the Monstrous Regiment of Women* (1558), in which he argued that 'to promote a woman to bear rule, superiority, dominion, or empire above any realm, nation, or city, is repugnant to nature; an insult to God, a thing most contrary to his revealed will and approved ordinance; and finally, it is the subversion of good order, of all equity and justice.'

Rosemary Radford Ruether (1936–): a pioneer of feminist theology who criticised traditional Christology as patriarchal and anti-Semitic. Ruether said we must go back to the Jesus tradition of the Gospels to find the resources for a feminist theology.

Tertullian (155–230): one of the earliest Christian theologians, he was infamous for the misogynistic views expressed in *On Female Fashion* and other works.

IDEAS

Androcentrism: taking maleness as normative.

Ecofeminism: the view that the oppression of women and the oppression of nature are interconnected.

First Wave feminism: the era of campaigns for women's rights, typified by the Suffragettes.

The hermeneutic of suspicion: an approach to the interpretation of Scripture and tradition that presumes the existence of oppression and exclusion. It has been used self-consciously by Schüssler Fiorenza in her critique of the Christian tradition.

Inclusive language: language that openly includes women.

Patriarchy (literally, 'the rule of the father'): a term that refers to a society ruled by men.

Phallocentrism: a term used to describe the priority given to the masculine in a culture or society.

Post-Christian feminism: the position, argued by Daphne Hampson and Mary Daly (in later years), that feminism must lead us beyond Christianity.

Post-feminism: a critique of feminism that blames some earlier feminist approaches for the continued oppression of women.

Second Wave feminism: a period (the late 1960s to the mid 1980s) in the history of feminism that was concerned with the transformation of the roles that women play in public and private life.

Third Wave feminism: a period (in the 1990s) of more philosophical feminism that focused on connecting feminist concerns with general and global questions of oppression and justice.

Womanist Theology: a distinct perspective that seeks to recognise, affirm and empower black women in determining the character of Christian religion.

BOOKS

Rosemary Radford Ruether, *Sexism and God-talk: Toward a Feminist Theology* (Beacon Press, 1983)

Lisa Isherwood and Dorothea McEwan (eds.), *An A to Z of Feminist Theology* (Sheffield Academic Press, 1996)

Stephanie Y. Mitchem, *Introducing Womanist Theology* (Orbis Books, 2002)

Imelda Whelehan, *Modern Feminist Thought from the Second Wave to 'Post Feminism'* (Edinburgh University Press, 1995)

Fundamentalism

A term that refers to religions or other social groups that demand strict and literal adherence to a sacred text or dogmatic principles.

The term 'fundamentalism' was first used to describe the conservative Protestants' strict adherence to what they regarded as the literal reading of the Bible. Now we speak of fundamentalisms of all kinds – secular and religious.

Fundamentalism is the belief in an absolute authority, normally derived from a literal reading of a sacred text. Fundamentalisms have an overriding concern with authority, law and rule-based ethics. For fundamentalists the question of truth is not vague or uncertain: the truth has been revealed in an unambiguous way and any questioning of the truth must be a form of heresy. Fundamentalisms are generally male-dominated, anti-gay, racist and xenophobic.

A basic feature of fundamentalist religion is the control of official teaching, which is handed down by the religious hierarchy. In Christian fundamentalism, for example, there is no scope for the individual believer to deviate from the doctrine of substitutionary atonement – although this doctrine is only one interpretation of the biblical texts. The fundamentalist model does not allow for any other view than the official one. Exploration of alternatives is treated as apostasy.

In the modern period it became commonplace for people to talk about the decline of religion. Marx believed that Christianity would simply wither away as socialism lifted the scales from the eyes of the proletariat. In the 1960s even Christian theologians started to talk about 'religionless Christianity' and 'secular Christianity'. But Christianity has refused to conform with the prophecies of its demise. While liberal churches have indeed declined, fundamentalist churches have thrived. It seems that the advance of secular humanism has not been welcomed by everyone.

It is a puzzle to know why, in an age saturated with secular and anti-religious teaching, fundamentalisms of many kinds have flourished in the major world religions. It is perhaps too simple to say that in an age of post-modern insecurity, unstable identities and uncertain truths, fundamentalism offers a consoling security – although this is probably partly true. Karen Armstrong argues that fundamentalism is a deeper response to modernity and secularism: 'Fundamentalists feel that they are battling against forces that threaten their most sacred values ... Those who relish the freedoms and achievements of modernity find it hard to understand the distress they cause religious fundamentalists.'

Others – such as Slavoj Zizek – have suggested that the rise of fundamentalism can be accounted for by Freud's theory of 'the return of the repressed'. Repressed psychological material does not disappear, but resurfaces in a displaced form in neurotic or psychotic behaviour. According to this analogy, the growth in fundamentalism represents the return of basic religious behaviour which had been suppressed by modern scientific thinking.

We tend to think of our age as one of increasing liberal democracy, global capitalism and scientific development. Following 9/11 and the growth in religious extremism, future generations may judge the phenomenon of fundamentalism to be the more significant. We live in an age, as Yeats put it in 'The Second Coming', when

> Things fall apart; the centre cannot hold;
> Mere anarchy is loosed upon the world,
> The blood-dimmed tide is loosed, and everywhere
> The ceremony of innocence is drowned;
> The best lack all conviction, while the worst
> Are full of passionate intensity.

THINKERS

Curtis Lee Laws (1868–46), editor of the Baptist journal, *The Watchman-Examiner*, invented the term 'fundamentalism' to describe certain conservative Protestant religions.

Slavoj Zizek (1949–) argues that fundamentalism is part of a pattern of global ideologies that includes liberal democracies as much as Middle-Eastern theocracies. In the West, argues Zizek, liberal democracy functions as our fundamentalism, our non-negotiable, absolute truth. And it is in the name of this democratic fundamentalism that the USA can invade other sovereign states, subvert normal standards of justice and commit acts of torture against its enemies. One of the unexamined dogmas of liberal democracy, argues Zizek, is its blind faith in capitalism.

IDEAS

Foundationalism: the view that knowledge is only possible if it stands upon a foundation of established truths or basic beliefs.

The Fundamentalism Project has gathered scholars from around the world to document and analyse the phenomenon of fundamentalism.

Pluralism: the belief that there is more than one version of the truth.

Relativism: the view that there are no absolute truths and that things are only true in a given cultural context.

BOOKS

Karen Armstrong, *The Battle for God: Fundamentalism in Judaism, Christianity and Islam* (HarperCollins, 2001)

Martin E. Marty and R. Scott Appleby (eds.), *Fundamentalisms Observed* (Chicago University Press, 1991)

Heaven and Hell

Heaven and hell are the mythical afterlife destinations for the saved and the damned respectively.

In the Old Testament, heaven and hell are only depicted sketchily. Hell was conceived of as 'Sheol' or 'a pit' of darkness; heaven was either thought of as the sky and the stars in the firmament, or in metaphors of celestial dwelling: a tent, or a pillared mansion. But the idea of heaven as future salvation only entered Jewish thought following the first exile (597 BC) and the destruction of the Temple. In captivity in Babylon, Jewish writers such as Isaiah started to dream of a 'New Jerusalem' and a restoration of the city and its people.

The concepts of 'heaven' and 'eternal punishment' (or hell) are firmly embedded in the New Testament. Jesus refers to 'heaven' as the place where God resides, and to 'the kingdom of heaven' as the arrival of heavenly rule upon the earth. Early Christian ideas of heaven were tied up with the apocalypse: the kingdom of heaven would arrive with Christ's second coming. The early Church, and probably Jesus himself, believed that the world would end imminently and that all humanity would be consigned to their final afterlife destinations.

According to New Testament mythology, heaven is also inhabited by angelic creatures and houses God's throne of judgement. The book of Revelation adds numerous other details, such as the 'pearly gates' of popular folklore.

Biblical ideas of heaven and hell depended upon a triple-decker cosmology with heaven above (the firmament), hell below (the underworld) and earth in between. God looks down, and speaks down, from heaven; and we are said to 'lift our eyes' to heaven to pray. Hell is an abyss beneath us where Christ is said to have 'descended' before the resurrection. At the end of his ministry, Jesus ascended into the sky, where heaven was thought to be.

Later Christian ideas of heaven became more mystical as the influences of abstract neo-Platonic ideas of paradise came to bear on theology. Heaven became more ethereal and spiritual.

Modern Christians know that there is no heaven above or hell below, and do not believe in the triple-decker cosmos that was so real for Jesus and the first disciples. At best, the biblical schemes of heaven and hell must be understood mythologically. Heaven may be thought of as the after-effect of our life on those who are left behind, or as a hope for the transformation of the earth, or as a dimension of present experience. But the 'pie in the sky when you die' version of heaven is now only believable by naïve sentimentalists and hard-line biblical literalists.

For most Christians the idea of eternal punishment sits uneasily with the vision of a loving and merciful God. The most satisfactory ideas of hell are anthropological. As Oscar Wilde put it: 'We are each our own devil and we make this world our hell.'

The best that a modern person can, in good conscience, say about the idea that heaven and hell are 'real', is to be agnostic like Shakespeare, who said that the afterlife is 'the undiscovered country from whose bourn no traveller returns' (*Hamlet*). Perhaps there is more in heaven and earth than is dreamed of in our modern scientific cosmology – but we cannot know what it is.

THINKERS

Rudolf Bultmann (1884–1976) argued that 'there is no longer any heaven in the traditional sense of the word'. Heaven and hell are part of a mythology that must be understood existentially as 'the permanent futurity of God which is always there before man arrives' (from *Kerygma*). 'The real purpose of myth is not to present an objective picture of the world as it is but to express man's understanding of himself and the world in which he lives. Myth should be interpreted not cosmologically, but anthropologically, or better still existentially' (from *The New Testament and Mythology*).

Fyodor Dostoyevsky (1821–88): in Dostoyevsky's novel *The Brothers Karamazov*, Ivan Karamazov tells the twelfth-century parable of 'The Wanderings of Our Lady through Hell'. The Virgin Mary is so traumatised by a visit to hell that she begs God for mercy for the damned. 'How can I forgive his tormentors?' asks God, pointing to Jesus' wounds. Eventually she negotiates an annual amnesty from suffering in hell from Good Friday till Trinity Sunday.

Karl Marx (1818–83) criticised the Christian concept of heaven as an illusion of future reward which encourages people to endure their oppression and serves the interests of the ruling classes.

Plato (427–347 BC) thought of heaven or 'the Isles of the Blessed' as 'a region of purity, eternity, immortality and unchangeableness' (*Phaedo*). He is sometimes credited with inventing the idea of hell in his dialogue *The Gorgias*, where he speaks of a place of eternal punishment.

Jean-Paul Sartre (1905–80) suggested in his play *Huis Clos* ('No Exit') that hell comes about through the sado-masochistic experience of being with others: 'Garcin: So this is hell. I'd never have believed it. You remember all we were told about the torture-chambers, the fire and brimstone ... Old wives' tales! There's no need for red-hot pokers. Hell is other people.'

IDEAS

Elysium: in ancient Greek thought, the resting-place of the virtuous.

Hades: the ancient Greek underworld.

Limbo: the 'nicest' part of hell, where the unbaptised and virtuous non-believers go. The Roman Catholic Church has recently abolished the idea of limbo, saying that it was never official doctrine, although it was believed by St Augustine and St Thomas Aquinas.

Predestination: the idea that God has already sorted out in advance who will be going to heaven and who to hell.

Purgatory: a place where the saved go in order to be purified for heaven.

Sheol: the Jewish concept of hell as an underworld.

Tartarus: the lowermost part of hell, beneath Hades.

BOOKS
Peter Stanford, *Heaven* (HarperCollins, 2002)
Alice Turner, *The History of Hell* (Harvest Books,1995)

Heresy

Traditionally, any Christian teaching that is contrary to the orthodox doctrines of the Church.

Because the Church has traditionally believed itself to be in possession of absolute truths handed directly down from God himself, heresy (or deviation from Church teaching) has been regarded as an act of defiance against God. As promulgators of false teaching, heretics have been regarded as dangerous and corrupting. Consequently the Church has shunned those whom it regards as heretics, and on many occasions heretics have been executed. Indeed, St Thomas Aquinas argued that death should be the standard punishment for heresy.

The word 'heresy' comes from a Greek word that means 'to choose', implying that the heretic merely makes up his own teachings rather than accepting the official truths of the Church. In our own modern and pluralistic age, most people would now agree with Graham Greene that being a heretic implies an admirable independence of mind: 'heresy is another word for freedom of thought'. The heretic is one who stands up against doctrinaire attitudes, religious intolerance, the repression of individual freedoms and theological arrogance.

Compared with the later history of Christianity, the early Church was liberal in its attitude to heresy. Heretical sects (some of which are listed below) were argued against vociferously, but it was not thought necessary to put them to death. Indeed, the more liberal Church Fathers like Justyn Martyr recognised that truth was possible outside the Church. The punishment for heresy in the early Church was excommunication, which may not have been very pleasant, but was much more preferable to the punishments that would become common treatment in the medieval and early modern periods.

From the fourth century, the Church became entwined with the secular power of the Roman Empire, and the treatment of heresy became an official crime that required judicial procedures and punishment. This culminated in the establishment of the Inquisition in the thirteenth century. The Inquisition actively sought out heretics, put them on trial and handed out punishment. One of its most celebrated victims was Giordano Bruno, the Renaissance philosopher and Dominican monk. The charges against Bruno are not known, but he was imprisoned for eight years and burnt at the stake in 1600.

The persecution of heretics was not only a Roman Catholic phenomenon. For example, in 1553 Michael Servetus, a distinguished scientist, was burnt at the stake at the personal insistence of John Calvin for not affirming the doctrine of the Trinity. An argument offered in mitigation for this shameful aspect of Church history is that the Church was merely acting by the standards of the day, and that extreme physical punishment was acceptable practice in medieval Europe. This argument probably has some merit. But we must surely question an organisation that for 600 years was prepared to commit and sanction torture and murder in the name of a God of love.

THINKERS

Tertullian (155–230) wrote a short essay against heresies, saying that the Christian truth is not something 'chosen' by us, but an indisputable teaching handed down from the apostles: 'We ... are not permitted to cherish any object after our own will, nor yet to make choice of that which another has introduced of his private fancy. In the Lord's apostles we possess our authority; for even they ... faithfully delivered ... the doctrine which they had received from Christ' (*The Prescription against Heretics*).

St Thomas Aquinas (1226–74). In his *Summa Theologica* Aquinas justified the death penalty for heresy: 'As for heretics, their sin deserves banishment, not only from the Church by excommunication, but also from this world by death. To corrupt the faith, whereby the soul lives, is much graver than to counterfeit money, which supports temporal life. Since forgers and other malefactors are summarily condemned to death by the civil authorities, with much more reason may heretics as soon as they are convicted of heresy be not only excommunicated, but also justly be put to death' (2:2:3:11). Apologists for Aquinas argue that the death penalty was a standard form of punishment in his age.

IDEAS

Anathema: the state of being excommunicated. 'If any one preaches a gospel besides that which you have received, let him be anathema' (St Paul, Gal. 1:9).

Apostasy: the abandonment of the Christian faith in favour of some other religion or belief-system.

Arianism: an early Christian sect inspired by Arius, who denied the divinity of Christ.

Blasphemy: the act of defaming God.

Doceticism: teaching that denied the humanity of Jesus.

Donatists: a heretical North African sect who refused to accept the ministry of those clergy who had renounced their faith during the persecution of the Church by the Roman Emperor Diocletian.

Excommunication: punitive expulsion from the Church.

Heterodoxy: teaching that varies from the official teaching of the Church.

Infidel: a member of a non-Christian religion. For many centuries the archetypal 'infidels' were the Jews, who were regarded not only as wilfully perverse in their refusal to accept Jesus but also responsible for his crucifixion. In recent times, extreme conservative Christians have focused their animosity towards infidels on Islam.

Maleficia: the offence of practising witchcraft.

Malleus maleficarum (or *The Hammer of Witches*, published by the Inquisition in 1485–86): a misogynistic text that linked all evil to women: 'Women are by nature instruments of Satan. They are by nature carnal, a structural defect rooted in the original creation.'

Orthodoxy: the official teaching of the Church.

Pelagianism: the teaching of Pelagius that Adam's original sin did not corrupt humanity but merely set us a bad example.

Perfidy: a breach of faith.

The Inquisition: a body set up in 1232 by the Roman Catholic Church to bring legal proceedings and judicial punishment to heretics. The Inquisition toured the country demanding repentance from alleged 'heretics'. If the victims repented, they received a minor punishment. Those who refused to confess and repent were often tortured and – if found guilty – fined, imprisoned or killed. It is difficult to estimate how many people died at the hands of the Inquisition.

Witch-hunts: Although heresy was often the 'legal' charge against witches, the social, political and psychological motivation for witch-hunts was more complex. Between the fourteenth and sixteenth centuries, witches were blamed for the spread of the plague and were persecuted in hysterical, fear-driven purges. The persecution of witches often involved brutal torture to extract confessions. Systematic witch-hunts continued until the late seventeenth century. In 1692 the infamous Salem Witch Trial resulted in 20 executions. Matthew Hopkins, the so-called 'Witch-Finder General', was responsible for possibly 200 executions in East Anglia between 1644 and 1646. Jane Wenham, the last convicted witch in England, was sentenced to death in 1712. The total number of witches murdered in the European persecutions is difficult to determine, and estimates range from 40,000 to 100,000.

BOOKS

G. R. Evans, *A Brief History of Heresy* (Blackwells, 2003)
Rowan Williams, *Arius: Heresy and Tradition* (SCM Press, 2001)

Hermeneutics

Hermeneutics is the study of interpretation, both of texts and of life itself.

The word 'hermeneutics', meaning the science of interpretation, comes from 'Hermes', the name of the messenger to the Greek gods. The question of how the Bible should be interpreted has always been crucial to Christianity, and hermeneutics soon became an important part of Christian theology. For example, the early theologian Origen devised a scheme of interpretation which distinguished between the literal, ethical and allegorical meanings of Scripture.

But since the beginning of the nineteenth century hermeneutics has assumed a central place in Christian theology. The Enlightenment challenged the historical truth of Scripture: the reality of miracles, the existence of God and the truth of the biblical account of creation. This forced biblical scholars to develop a new, more 'scientific' approach to interpreting Scripture. This became known as 'the historical–critical method', which attempted to uncover both the historical basis of Scripture and the history of the construction of the biblical texts. As a result, theologians started to distinguish between the historical (true) and mythical (made-up) components of Scripture. In addition, liberal theologians started to ask again about the religious truth of Scripture and how the Christian message should be interpreted for our contemporary context.

The nineteenth-century development of textual hermeneutics extended into the twentieth century, not only with the emergence of new forms of textual analysis – form criticism, redaction criticism and structuralism – but with the development of 'existential hermeneutics', which studied how we interpret life itself. Martin Heidegger, for example, argued that the interpretation of our own personal existence (the so-called 'Question of Being') is what makes us human, since animals do not enquire into the significance of their lives.

The distinction between 'textual' and 'existential' (or 'philosophical') hermeneutics is useful, but we have to be careful of making this distinction too clear cut. Some theologians (for example, D. Z. Phillips and Don Cupitt) argue that life itself is completely textual in nature; and there are others (for example, Paul Ricoeur) who argue that texts can only be interpreted in the light of our human existence.

At the centre of all hermeneutics is a 'problem' which is sometimes called 'the hermeneutic circle'. Because we all exist in time, our understanding is continually being changed by experience. As we change, our interpretations of texts and life also change. Interpretation is a never-ending circle of interactions between ourselves and our world. So, for example, the biblical stories take on quite new meanings as we grow older and have new life-experiences. Furthermore, this endless cycle of interpretation is simultaneously happening in different ways for different people. As Kierkegaard exclaimed: 'And then the interpretations – 30,000 different interpretations!'

The hermeneutic problem appears to make true and final interpretations impossible. Karl Barth's response is to say that God solves the problem of hermeneutics through the Holy Spirit, who interprets everything for us, as it says in the hymn: 'Blind unbelief is sure to err and scan His work in vain,/ God is his own interpreter and he will make it plain.' For others, such as John Dominic Crossan, the ambiguity and plurality of interpretation is taken as a positive virtue. He says that Jesus' parables are intended precisely to subvert 'religion that gives one final "word" about reality'.

The challenge of hermeneutics is to provide an account of interpretation which is faithful to the plurality of possible meanings but, at the same time, faithful to the quest for truth. The current consensus, which brings together liberals such as David Tracy and conservatives such as Stanley Hauerwas, is that narrative provides the best model for understanding a truth which has many perspectives and which unfolds over time.

THINKERS

Rudolf Bultmann (1844–1976) argued that we must 'demythologise' the biblical texts in order to reveal their essential message or *kerygma* (Greek for 'preaching').

Wilhelm Dilthey (1833–1911) argued that interpretation must be grounded in the 'lived experience' (*Erlebnis*) of the individual.

Hans-Georg Gadamer (1900–2002) argued in *Truth and Method* that all our interpretations are 'prejudiced' by our place in history and culture. So the task of interpretation is to distinguish between our true and false prejudices. We achieve this by a method that Gadamer called the 'fusion of horizons' in which we engage in a 'conversation' with the thing being interpreted. It is in the course of this conversation that our prejudices get 'played out' and the truth emerges.

D. Z. Phillips (1934–2006) used Wittgenstein's later philosophy to argue that religion is a 'language game' that can only be understood within the 'form of life' in which religious language is used.

Paul Ricoeur (1913–2005) argued that human existence is essentially narrative in nature and that we must understand life in terms of its historical and fictional stories.

Friedrich Schleiermacher (1768–1834): the pioneer of modern hermeneutics who followed Herder in arguing that we must try to understand the original context of a text and the mind of its author. There are two aspects to interpretation: a 'comparative' approach which looks at all the contexts and the objective data; and a 'divinatory' approach which is subjective and intuitive.

Albert Schweitzer (1875–1965) wrote the world's best-known book about the Jesus of history, *The Quest for the Historical Jesus*. Schweitzer argued that Jesus was an eschatological prophet who expected the world to come to an imminent end.

Ludwig Wittgenstein (1889–1951): a philosopher of religion who argued that all human life must be understood within systems of language that he called 'language games'.

IDEAS

Deconstruction: a form of post-structuralism, pioneered by Jacques Derrida, that seeks to demonstrate that there are no definitive meanings in either texts or life in general.

Exegesis: the process of interpretation that tries to draw out the meaning of a text.

Form Criticism: a technique of biblical criticism, devised by Herman Gunkel, that tries to understand the cultural setting (*Sitz im Leben*) within which an oral or written text would have been first written and used.

The hermeneutic circle: a concept invented by Schleiermacher to describe the unending process of interpretation (see above).

The hermeneutic of suspicion: an approach to texts that assumes the suppression of the voices of disempowered groups.

The historical–critical method: the dominant approach to Scripture since the early nineteenth century, which tries to establish the historical truth behind the biblical texts.

New Criticism: post-war literary criticism, associated with William Empson and Northrop Frye, which emphasised the plurality and ambiguity of all textual interpretations.

New Hermeneutics: a name for the post-war revival of interest in hermeneutics represented by thinkers such as Rudolf Bultmann and Ernst Fuchs.

Post-structuralism: a philosophical outlook that regards all textual structures and codes as unstable.

Reader-response Criticism: an approach to interpretation that says the individual reader's understanding of a text is always true.

Redaction Criticism: an approach to biblical criticism that tries to detect the roles and attitudes of the editors of the scriptural material.

Structuralism: the analysis of texts in terms of their basic structures and codes of meaning.

BOOKS

Anthony C. Thiselton, *The Two Horizons: New Testament Hermeneutics and Philosophical Description* (Eerdmans, 1980)

Francis Watson, *Text, Church and World: Biblical Interpretation in Theological Perspective* (Edinburgh, 1994)

Incarnation

The doctrine that God became human in Jesus Christ.

The incarnation (the word comes from a Latin term meaning 'to enflesh') is the doctrine that, in Jesus Christ, God 'took flesh' to become a human being. At the heart of the incarnation is a paradox: how God and a human being can be one (see 'Christology'). The rational explanations of the doctrine soon give way to mystery.

In Christian visual art the reality of the incarnation is often emphasised by depicting Christ's nakedness and physicality: the contours of his body, his wounds, his blood. Andrea Mantegna's *Crucifixion*, for example, shows Christ with a body identical to those of the two thieves beside him. Rubens' *Crucifixion* shows the soldiers straining under the weight of Christ's physical body to lift the cross into its vertical position.

Broadly speaking, we can distinguish between restricted and

general theologies of the incarnation. The restricted versions of the incarnation argue that God became flesh exclusively in the person of Jesus. Karl Barth, for example, regarded the incarnation as a one-off event, a unique revelation of God in Jesus that cannot be understood apart from an encounter with Christ. By contrast, a general theology of the incarnation, such as that offered by Pierre Teilhard de Chardin, argues that although the incarnation is focused and rooted in Jesus, the mystic reality of the incarnation is everywhere in the cosmos. The world is 'a divine milieu' and the incarnation is the presence of the Godhead in every moment of our existence. As Gerard Manley Hopkins put it: 'Christ plays in ten thousand places'.

The mystics have tended to emphasise the reality of the incarnation as present within the believer. Meister Eckhart argued that the incarnation must be real within us: 'What good is it to me if this eternal birth of the divine Son takes place unceasingly but does not take place within myself?' Eckhart's views were condemned in a papal bull of 1329. St Bonaventure's meditation on the 'Five Feasts of the Child Jesus' says that we must mystically 'give birth to Christ' in our lives.

The idea that other people carry with them the reality of Christ became a central theological insight in 'Socialist' Christian ethics. For example, the nineteenth-century Christian Socialist Stewart Hedlam argued that 'you are literally … feeding, clothing, housing Jesus Christ when you are feeding, clothing, housing any human being.'

The theology of the incarnation has been at the centre of the recent interest in the 'theology of the body' (see also 'Soul') and theologies of sexuality. The incarnation means that Christ must have been a sexual being, dealing with all the normal aspects of human physicality. In Christ, the human body – in all its aspects – became something sacred.

THINKERS

Thomas Altizer (1927–) has argued that the incarnation should be understood as a cosmic affirmation of the world of the flesh and human history. By becoming human, God collapses the distinction between the sacred and the profane: 'Christian theology must affirm the union of the sacred into the profane and affirm the profane as profane.'

Nikos Kazantzakis (1883–1957): a Greek Christian philosopher whose book *The Last Temptation of Christ* explored the more radical sexual implications of the incarnation. If God truly became flesh, then he must also have been a sexual being. Kazantzakis saw the incarnation as fundamental to his view of life. Elsewhere he wrote: 'within me even the most metaphysical problem takes on a warm physical body which smells of sea, soil, and human sweat. The Word, in order to touch me, must become warm flesh. Only then do I understand – when I can smell, see, and touch.'

Maurice Merleau-Ponty (1908–61): a French philosopher who explored the relationship between the twin human experiences of being 'conscious' and being a body of 'flesh'. Merleau-Ponty describes the experience of touching oneself as a form of self-consciousness: a realisation that we are all incarnate beings, and that the incarnation of God in Christ is just a special case of the general human condition.

Michel Henry (1922–2002): a French phenomenological theologian who explored the theme of incarnation in his book *Incarnation, a philosophy of the flesh*. For Henry, our experience is a complex combination of our inner awareness of having a body and the external encounter with our own bodies. This self-conscious awareness of our own flesh and the flesh of others is quite different from the experience of mere matter, and is the fundamental revelation of the reality of Life. In the incarnation God becomes 'flesh', as we are, and not merely a physical body. So the *Logos*, the Word of God, reveals itself as Life. The incarnation is 'the auto-affection of Life': God celebrating and loving the Life which is his.

IDEAS

Avatara: the Hindu concept that the gods occasionally take human or animal form.

Sarx: the Greek word for 'flesh' used in New Testament.

Logos: see separate section.

BOOKS

Jeremy Begbie (ed.), *Beholding the Glory: Incarnation Through the*

Arts (Baker Academic, 2000)

John Hick, *The Metaphor of God Incarnate: Christology in a Pluralistic Age* (Westminster/John Knox, 1993)

Brian Hebblethwaite, *The Incarnation: Collected Essays in Christology* (CUP, 1987)

Inclusive Theology

Theology that emphasises the openness of God towards all creation and values such as hospitality, generosity and acceptance.

A basic issue in Christian theology since the earliest times has been the question of who should be included in (and who should be excluded from) the Church. This issue has come to the fore in recent decades over questions such as the role of women, lesbians and gay men within the Church, and whether non-Christian religions can also lead people to God.

But our current concerns need to be understood in terms of the wider history of inclusive theology. It is not, as its detractors argue, a modern invention, but a crucial strand in Christian thinking since the earliest times.

The issue of inclusion first arises in the pages of the New Testament. Jesus, in conversation with a Syro-Phoenician woman (Mark 7), appears to say that his ministry is only for the Jews, but is persuaded to reach out to a gentile woman and her child. The early Church also faced a fundamental issue of inclusion, which is recorded in Galatians 2. Hitherto the Church had seen itself as an offshoot of Judaism and had retained many Jewish customs, including circumcision. St Paul argued successfully that the essence of Christianity is faith in Jesus, not conformity to traditions and regulations. Thus the Church took an historic step towards greater inclusion, accepting the full membership of non-Jews.

The early Church also had to wrestle with the question of those who had died before the birth of Christ. These people had not heard the teaching of Jesus and were apparently unfairly excluded from salvation. The first letter of Peter imagines that Christ preached to the imprisoned souls of the dead, giving them a chance to accept salvation. This explanation may not sound very believable to modern ears, but it reflects the inclusive instincts of the earliest Christian theologians.

In the second and third centuries the Church faced the question of inclusion again, this time in disputes with the Gnostics about the theology of creation. Whereas the Gnostics saw the world as divided into good and evil, Irenaeus and Augustine argued that everything created by God is necessarily good. This was an extremely difficult case to make when the world clearly appears to contain both good and bad people, suffering and happiness. But the Church Fathers resisted the Gnostics tooth and nail, knowing that a dualistic view of creation could easily be used to demonise whole categories of 'evil' people and thereby justify violence against them. The orthodoxy that prevailed insisted on a radically inclusive view of creation and the inherent goodness of every creature.

Augustine was inclusive on another major theological issue. He argued against the Donatists, a hard-line sect who would have no truck with those Christian clergy who had renounced their faith during the persecution of the Church by the Emperor Diocletian (303–305). Augustine pleaded successfully for forgiveness, and argued that the office of errant ministers could not be invalidated by their personal conduct.

His inclusive outlook can be found elsewhere in the writings of the Church Fathers. Justin Martyr argued that human reason can guide non-Christians to God; Irenaeus emphasised the universalism (catholicity) of the Christian Church and its appeal to all people, not just the select few; Origen believed that all people (even the devil) would be saved by God's mercy in the fullness of time.

In the modern period the most important inclusive theologian was Karl Rahner, who argued that it is possible for anyone to be an 'anonymous Christian': 'Anonymous Christianity means that a person lives in the grace of God and attains salvation outside of explicitly constituted Christianity … Let us say, a Buddhist monk … who, because he follows his conscience, attains salvation and lives in the grace of God; of him I must say that he is an anonymous Christian' (*Karl Rahner in Dialogue: Conversations and Interviews 1965–1982*, Crossroad, 1986, p. 15).

In the face of contemporary Gnosticism and exclusivism, the task for inclusive theology is to keep articulating the historic teaching of the Church: that all humanity is created in God's image; that God's grace and forgiveness are limitless; that human love and reason are both universal and God-given; and that God's vision for the future is an inclusive community that Jesus called 'the kingdom'.

THINKERS

James Alison (1959–): a gay, Roman Catholic theologian powerfully influenced by René Girard. Alison sees the issue of inclusion in the context of a theology of human brokenness and violence. All humanity is included both in the reality of original sin and in the reality of God's forgiveness, exemplified in the resurrection.

Justin Martyr (100?–165?) argued for the inclusion of Socrates and other ancient thinkers who were able to understand Christ as Logos without knowing Jesus personally.

St Paul (3–65) argued that the 'unknown god' intuited by the Athenians was the same as the Christian God (Acts 17:23), thereby providing the theological basis for a faith that includes even those who are not confessing Christians.

Francis Petrarch (1304–74): a Renaissance poet whose poem *Africa* provoked controversy about Christian inclusiveness. Petrarch was criticised for making the speech of a Carthaginian character called 'Mago' too Christian. Petrarch offered a passionate defence: 'What, I pray, is Christian here, and not simply universally human? ... What else but grief and lamentation and remorse of a man at the point of death? ... one does not have to be a Christian to recognise one's errors and sins and feel shame and remorse ... A Christian knows whom to confess his faults, and how to confess them; but awareness of them and the pricks of conscience and repentance and self-accusation – all that is within the capacity of any rational being.'

IDEAS

Feminist theology: see separate entry.

Gender-inclusive language: the use of language that does not exclude or demean women: for example, using 'Godself' instead of 'himself' as the reflexive pronoun for God.

General revelation: a term used to describe the revelation which is accessible to everyone, of every religion and none.

Lesbian and gay theology: theology arising out of the experience of lesbians and gay men.

Liberation theology: see separate entry.

Queer theology: theology that challenges all received norms in gender and sexuality.

BOOKS

Steven Shakespeare and Hugh Rayment-Pickard, *The Inclusive God*, (SCM/Canterbury Press, 2006)

Elizabeth Stuart, *Lesbian and Gay Theologies* (Ashgate, 2003)

Kairos

A view of time as a series of moments or opportunities.

Kairos is an ancient Greek term used by Jesus and St Paul to mean 'the right time'. The early Church, and Jesus himself, believed that the end of the world was imminent and that Jesus' appearance was the *kairos* moment around which the fate of the cosmos would turn.

In ancient thought Kairos was a mythical figure: a young man, usually naked, with winged feet and long hair hanging over his face. In some cases he is shown fleeing from a crowd who are trying to grasp him by the forelock. Kairos is often depicted carrying a pair of scales to show that we must use our judgement in order to make the best of life's fleeting opportunities, because time is a series of windows for human decision, action and responsibility. There was, we are told, a statue to Kairos outside the stadium at Olympia. This was a reminder to the athletes to 'seize their moment'.

In the Bible the concept of kairos is contrasted with the view of time as *chronos*. *Chronos* is clock time, the sweep of events from past to future. *Kairos* is the opposite of chronos: it is not time in general, but particular moments of time – the 'hours', 'days', 'seasons' of history. If *chronos* refers to time as a continuous line, then *kairos* refers to specific points on the line. The most famous description of *kairos* time in the Old Testament is the passage in Ecclesiates 3 that says there is a 'season for everything, and a time for every matter under heaven ... a time to weep, and a time to laugh; a time to mourn, and a time to dance ... God has made everything beautiful in its time.' So the wisdom of time is knowing what each moment is for.

When Jesus talks about time, he uses the word *kairos* rather than *chronos*. In the Sermon on the Mount, for example, he tells us to take each day as it comes: 'Consider the lilies of the field, how they grow; they neither toil nor spin' (Matt. 6:28). But Jesus also uses *kairos* to refer to the importance of his own appearance in human history: his life, death and resurrection is a *kairos*, a unique opportunity for humanity, if only we have the wisdom to seize it.

The view of time as *kairos*, or special moments of significance, is common among mystics and poets. Jean Pierre de Caussade's concept of 'the sacrament of the present moment' described grace in terms of God's gift to us of time. T. S. Eliot and R. S. Thomas were both fascinated by the idea of time as the present moment.

For the existentialists also, the immediate present was significant as the place where human existence happens. Søren Kierkegaard wrote about the importance of the moment of existential decision, an idea which Martin Heidegger developed into his own 'moment of vision' (*Augenblick*) when our existential situation becomes clear to us.

The view of time as *kairos* is now extremely widespread both in New Age religions and in popular Christian spirituality. A recent book by Eckhart Tolle called *The Power of Now* was an international best-seller. This fits in with the general trend in late capitalist cultures towards individualised and privatised religion.

THINKERS

Aristotle (384–322 bc) argued that the moving 'now' is the basis of all time.

St Augustine (354–430) was the first Christian theologian to attempt a theology of time. In his *Confessions* Augustine concluded that the past and the future are not real and that the only real time is 'the present'. However, since the present can always be divided into a smaller duration, he concluded that 'the present' cannot be determined. Thus time is a mystery that only God can fathom.

Jean-Pierre de Caussade (1675–1751): an eighteenth-century Jesuit whose *Self-abandonment to Divine Providence* put forward the doctrine of 'the sacrament of the present moment': 'What God ordains for each moment is what is most holy, best and most divine for us. All we need to know is how to recognise his will in the present moment.'

T. S. Eliot (1888–1965): a Christian poet whose *Four Quartets* affirms the vision of history as 'a pattern of timeless moments'.

R. S. Thomas (1913–2000): a Welsh priest and poet who saw 'the moment' as a special aspect of time: 'the moment is history's navel and round it the worlds spin'. For Thomas the task of religion is to find 'love's moment in a world in servitude to time'.

Lysippos of Sikyon (fourth century BC): a sculptor whose statue of Kairos carried this epigram: '"And who are you, Kairos, who subdues all things, and why do you stand on tip-toe?" "I am ever running."'

Friedrich Nietzsche (1844–1900) regarded the whole of the cosmos as a series of moments in an endless circulation which he called 'the eternal return of the same'.

IDEAS

Epiphany: a Greek word meaning a moment of disclosure or 'showing'. 'Epiphany' is used in a religious sense to describe a moment of divine revelation – and the appearance of the magi at Bethlehem is referred to as The Epiphany. But others, such as James Joyce, have used 'epiphany' in a secular sense to mean a moment of perception and insight.

Phronesis: a term, coined by the Greek philosopher Isocrates, for the 'practical insight' required to use each opportunity in life to the best advantage. As Cicero put it, 'In an oration, as in life, nothing is harder to determine than what is appropriate.'

BOOKS

Phillip Sipora and James Baumlin (eds.), *Rhetoric and Kairos: Essays in History, Theory and Praxis* (State University of New York Press, 2002)

Hugh Rayment-Pickard, *The Myths of Time* (DLT, 2004)

Liberal Theology

Liberal theology emphasises the importance of reason, individualism and human freedom.

The term 'liberal theology' is generally used to describe a very specific trend in theology which followed the rational and scientific developments of the Enlightenment.

For many in the age of the Enlightenment, it felt as if (to use Kant's phrase) human beings were at last 'growing up' and uncovering the real truth about the world and our place in it. In particular, Newton's achievements in science had dazzled the whole of Europe. As Alexander Pope famously put it: 'God said, Let Newton be! and all was light.' The sciences made religious belief look obsolete and superstitious.

Rather than simply restating the traditional faith, nineteenth-century liberal Protestant theologians tried to modernise Christian theology to make it intelligible and acceptable to this new 'enlightened' culture. In biblical scholarship, critics like D. F. Strauss and H. Paulus subjected the biblical texts to 'scientific' analysis, trying to uncover the 'facts' beneath layers of myth and superstition. (See 'Biblical Criticism'.) Schleiermacher defended Christianity against its Enlightenment critics, arguing that religion is not a system of knowledge which can be 'disproved' by reason, but an intuitive feeling-reaction to the wonder and magnitude of the cosmos. Albrecht Ritschl followed Kant in seeing Christian faith as essentially ethical and concerned with human 'value judgements'. Paul Tillich, writing in the twentieth century, said that theology must begin with questions of human existence. In general, the liberal theologians tried to make theology more worldly, less metaphysical, more rooted in human experience. As Harvey Cox, a 1960s liberal, put it: 'we speak of God to secular man by speaking about man.'

In the twentieth century there was a powerful backlash against liberal theology. Karl Barth was, and remains, the figurehead of anti-liberal sentiment. He argued that God cannot be understood in human categories, and that we must submit to God's will and accept his sovereign Word. The Church must not accommodate itself to human culture – not even Enlightenment culture – but must articulate with authority the distinctive Christian message. Barth's anti-liberal banner has been carried by a number of theologians since, notably in recently years by Stanley Hauerwas.

The current consensus about the failings of liberal theology has made the word 'liberal' almost unusable, except as a term of abuse, in some church circles. Liberal theology is taken to be the self-defeating attempt to save Christianity by betraying its unique identity. Hauerwas, for example, credits liberal theology with the destruction of Christianity.

So-called 'post-liberal' theologians now argue that the modernist, Enlightenment paradigm is collapsing and that any theology based on Enlightenment values must also collapse. As people search for new values and a new world-view, there will be opportunities for Christian renewal, if the churches can remain faithful to the historic Christian message.

However, the critique of liberal theology does not work so well if we acknowledge that the history of liberal Christianity goes back beyond the Enlightenment to the New Testament itself. There were many liberals before the nineteenth century. The latitudinarian Anglicans had strong liberal instincts, as did Renaissance theologians such as Ficino and Petrarch. The Christian mystics – for example, John of the Cross, Meister Eckhardt and Nicholas of Cusa – emphasised the primacy of spiritual experience over doctrinal purity. Justyn Martyr argued for the centrality of reason in faith. And St Paul, despite popular misconceptions, was a liberal, arguing for the equality of slaves and women, and insisting that the Christian truth lies in the spirit of Christian life and not in the words of Christian dogma.

THINKERS

Joseph Glanvill (1636–80): an English clergyman and philosopher who attacked dogma and championed science. He wrote: 'The belief of our Reason is an exercise of Faith: and our Faith is an act of Reason.' 'The denial of reason in religion hath been the principal engine that heretics have used against the faith.'

Adolf von Harnack (1851–1930) argued in *The Essence of Christianity* that Jesus taught a simple Gospel of essential truths which was distorted by St Paul and other theologians into unnecessarily complex doctrines and rigid dogmas.

Stanley Hauerwas (1940–): the most robust and celebrated living critic of liberal theology. He argues that it is simply 'disguised humanism': 'I claim that Christianity has died as a result of its love affair with liberal democracy. I think that liberal democracy, in many ways, took as its fundamental task to kill Christianity by domesticating its strongest views.'

Immanuel Kant (1724–1804) argued that God must be understood as an ethical and aesthetic ideal.

John Locke (1632–1704): an English empiricist philosopher who argued for the importance of reason in religion (*The Reasonableness of Christianity*).

Justyn Martyr (100–165) argued that Christ is the *Logos* or rational principle behind all creation, and that the worship of Christ was therefore a supremely reasonable act.

Albrecht Ritschl (1822–89) saw God's love, shown in Jesus Christ, as the basis of our human efforts to transform society.

Friedrich Schleiermacher (1768–1834) tried to defend Christianity against its 'cultured despisers' in the Enlightenment era, representing theology in terms of a human 'sense of absolute dependence' upon God.

Ernst Troeltsch (1865–1923) argued that Christianity is concerned with individual religious life and the human social order.

Edward Young (1683–1765) commented in his *Night Thoughts* that religion is 'the proof of common sense'.

IDEAS

Aufklärung: the German word for 'enlightenment' used by Kant.

Latitudinarianism: a seventeenth-century English liberal approach to theology, typified by Archbishop John Tillotson (1630–94). Latitudinarians emphasised reason over authority in theology.

Post-liberal theology: a term coined by George Lindbeck to describe theology after the collapse of modern liberal ideology. Post-liberal theology is criticised for having no guiding identity except its rejection of 'liberal theology'.

BOOKS

Gary Dorrien, *The Making of American Liberal Theology: Imagining Progressive Religion: 1805–1900* (Westminster/John Knox, 2002)

Gary Dorrien, *The Making of American Liberal Theology: Idealism, Realism and Modernity: 1900–1950* (Westminster/John Knox, 2003)

Gary Dorrien, *The Making of American Liberal Theology: Crisis, Irony, and Postmodernity: 1950–2005* (Westminster/John Knox, 2006)

Liberation Theology

Theology that identifies with the experience, needs and struggles of the poor and oppressed.

Liberation theology originated in Roman Catholic communities in Latin America in the 1960s out of the struggles of the poor against oppression and social injustice. From these origins it has developed into a political theology which has been applied to the experience of many oppressed groups, including women, lesbians and gays in the prosperous West.

Although liberation theology has drawn upon the theoretical insights of Marxism and twentieth-century Catholic social theology, the earliest liberation theology was rooted in the real experience of the struggles of the poor rather than in academic theology. The underlying conviction of liberation theology is that God is uniquely revealed in the lives of the oppressed:

> Christian poverty, and expression of love, is solidarity *with the poor* and is a protest *against poverty*. This is the concrete, contemporary meaning of the witness of poverty. It is a poverty lived not for its own sake, but rather as an authentic imitation of Christ; it is a poverty which means taking on the sinful human condition to liberate humankind from sin and all its consequences. (Gustavo Gutiérrez, *A Theology of Liberation*)

Christ was seen essentially as a 'liberator' with a political programme, the kingdom of God, which would deliver material freedom and justice, and not merely 'spiritual' benefits and abstract 'truth'. Indeed, 'liberation' and 'divinity' were seen as one and the same thing, so that any manifestation of freedom and justice became a divine revelation: 'wherever brotherhood, justice, liberation and goodness occur, there true Christianity becomes concrete and there lives the Gospel – even though it might be under an unnamed different banner' (Leonardo Boff).

However much it interested Western intellectuals, liberation theology never took root among the poor communities of First-World nations. And in the Latin American homelands of liberation theology, the poor are increasingly turning to Pentecostal churches. There is a consensus now that Latin American liberation theology is in crisis.

A basic weakness in Latin American liberation theology was its alignment with Marxism and socialism. As a consequence, its credibility was challenged severely by the collapse of Eastern European Marxist regimes in the late 1980s and early 1990s. Liberation theology never quite shrugged off its Catholic fondness for dogma. At the same time as liberation theologians were recognising the need to ground theology in human experience rather than doctrine, they were also aligning themselves with Marxist political ideology.

As a political theology, with the explicit aim of serving the poor, we might expect the main achievements of liberation theology to be improved material conditions for the poor. Despite its origins in practical political struggle, liberation theology has increasingly become an academic discipline, or an ideological 'stance'. One critic has summarised the achievements of liberation theology as enabling us to 'hear the voice of the poor'; 'opening up new ways of speaking about the political person'; and 'making a convincing case for the situatedness of all knowledge' (Rebecca Chopp in *The Modern Theologians*, Blackwell, 2005). These may be interesting intellectual outcomes, but they offer little comfort to the world's poor and oppressed.

The emergence of black theology, particularly in the United States, was a separate development, arising from the history of black people's oppression in North America and the Civil Rights and Black Power movements of the 1960s. Black theology connects black people's experience of racism and oppression with the Christian narrative. Of particular importance are the biblical narratives of liberation – for example, the story of the exodus of the oppressed Hebrew slaves from their captivity in Egypt. At the centre of black theology is the identification of Jesus as a black Christ challenging the white Christ of orthodox Christian mythology. The fact that Jesus of Nazareth was depicted as a white man in the Western Christian imagination is emblematic of a general racism present in European Christianity.

What liberation theologies have done best, and what they must keep doing, is to remind the churches and nations of their primary religious obligation to eradicate poverty, inequality and oppression.

THINKERS

Leonardo Boff (1938–): a Brazilian Franciscan and a leading liberation theologian who was suspended from duties and punished with 'obedient silence' by Pope John Paul II in 1985. In 1992, under threat of renewed censure from the Vatican, Boff gave up his role as a priest. In *Jesus Christ Liberator* Boff argues that we must discard 'the dogmatic Christ' in order to discover Christ as liberator of the poor.

Albert Cleage (1911–2000): pastor of the Shrine of the Black Madonna in Detroit. In his book *The Black Messiah* (1968) he argued that black Christians need to realise their identity as a 'Black Nation', rediscovering Jesus as 'a revolutionary black leader, a Zealot, seeking to lead a Black Nation to freedom.' Cleage adopted an African name: Jaramogi Abebe Agyeman, meaning 'liberator, holy man, saviour of the nation'.

Gustavo Gutiérrez (1928–): a Peruvian Dominican, regarded as the father of Latin American liberation theology. In *A Theology of Liberation* (1971) – the most influential work of liberation theology – Gutiérrez argued that theology must be a critical refection upon praxis.

Juan Luis Segundo (1925–96): a Jesuit priest and a founding figure in Latin American liberation theology. In *The Liberation of Theology* (1975) he argued that a radically new hermeneutic of liberation is required in theology. The interpretation of Scripture and tradition must transform and be transformed by both our material circumstances and our political commitments.

Martin Luther King (1929–68): the black civil rights leader who rejected the 'separatist' approach of the more radical black theologians, such as James Cone. In his famous 'I have a dream' address, King recommends a faith that 'will be able to transform the jangling discords of our nation into a beautiful symphony of brotherhood. With this faith we will be able to work together, to pray together, to struggle together, to go to jail together, to stand up for freedom together, knowing that we will be free one day.'

James Cone (1938–) is arguably the first theologian to offer a systematic expression of black theology. In *Black Theology and Black Power* (1969), he criticised not only the racism in societies but also the ways in which racism had been fostered by Christian thinking and practice.

Countée Cullen (1903–46): an African-American poet who in 'The Black Christ' compared the lynching of a black man to Christ's crucifixion, questioning the adequacy of a white Messiah: 'Christ who conquered Death and Hell/ What has he done for you who spent/ A bleeding life for his content?/ Or is the white Christ, too, distraught/ By these dark sins his Father wrought?'

IDEAS

Base communities: a form of church organisation that started in Latin America with small groups of poor Christians meeting to discuss Scripture in the light of their experiences of poverty and oppression.

Orthopraxis precedes orthodoxy: the idea that the correct practice of Christian ethics is more important than the correct articulation of doctrine.

Praxis: a term meaning what we actually do, rather than a theoretical perspective on what we do.

The preferential option for the poor: the idea that God shows particular concern and favour towards those in material poverty.

BOOKS

Leonardo Boff, *Introducing Liberation Theology* (Orbis, 1987)

Harvey Cox, *The Silencing of Leonardo Boff: Liberation Theology and the Future of World Christianity* (Meyer Stone & Co., 1988)

Christopher Rowland (ed.), *The Cambridge Companion to Liberation Theology* (CUP, 1999)

Gayraud Wilmore and James Cone, *Black Theology* (Orbis Books, 1980)

Logos

In Christian theology, the biblical term for Jesus as 'the Word' of God.

The concept of *Logos* has a long history with many meanings and uses, from the pre-Socratic philosophy of Heraclitus through to the present day. In classical Greek philosophy, *Logos* tends to mean both 'word' and 'reason', and is regarded as the governing, creative principle at work in structuring the cosmos.

In Christian theology the *Logos* is 'the Word of God', and the concept is used in various ways. The idea first appears in Scripture as God's creative word, a word-act that brings everything into existence (see Gen. 1:3; Ps. 32:9). For the Old Testament prophets, the 'word of God' was God's direct speech. Ezekiel, for example, writes that 'the word of the Lord came to [him]', and Jeremiah says that he speaks God's words. In Old Testament wisdom literature, the 'word' of God is associated with wisdom: 'O God of my Fathers and Lord of mercy, who has made all things by your word, and in your wisdom have formed man' (Wisd. 9:1–2).

Most significantly, 'the Word' or the Logos is how St John refers to Jesus in the dramatic opening verses of his Gospel: 'In the beginning was the Word and the Word was with God and the Word was God.' Jesus is the image and mind of God in living and breathing form.

The resonance with some Greek thought has led scholars to speculate that St John's concept of the *Logos* was influenced by Greek philosophy. In fact, the concept of *Logos* appears both in the Hebrew Scriptures (the Old Testament) and prominently in the writings of the Jewish philosopher Philo. Scholars now think that the theology in John's Gospel owes more to Jewish thought than to anything else.

For some of the early Christian theologians – for example: Tertullian, St Athanasius, Clement of Alexandria and Justin Martyr – the idea that Jesus was God's *Logos*, or the mind or image of God, provided the basis for understanding the two natures of Christ: the

Logos was the divine Christ who became flesh in the human Jesus. This view of the incarnation tied in nicely with dualistic Platonic ideas about the relationship between form and matter, soul and body.

The weakness with this approach was that it owed too much to Plato and gave too little importance to the physical dimension of Christ, implying that Christ's body was not an integral part of his identity but a temporary container for the eternal, divine *Logos*. Athanasius, for example, spoke about the Word 'assuming a body' in order to complete its work on earth. Alexandrian *Logos* theology also left little room for the desires and emotions that are also part of being fully human.

The prologue to John's Gospel associates the *Logos* with a range of concepts: life, grace, light, truth, power and glory. This constellation of concepts cannot simply be reduced to the rational forms of Platonic philosophy. Furthermore, John's Gospel insists that the *Logos* actually *became* flesh, rather than simply 'assuming' it. If John's Gospel is followed through to its conclusion, the final 'glory' of the *Logos* is the crucifixion – an event focused upon Christ's body and feelings.

Under the influence of Martin Heidegger (see below), twentieth-century Christian existentialists questioned the Alexandrian conception of the *Logos* as rational truth. Paul Tillich argued that the *Logos* is 'ontological reason', a Word that thinks and speaks out of the mystery of Being itself. The incarnation means that the *Logos* reveals itself not merely as an idea, but in the flesh of our historical existence.

THINKERS

St Athanasius (c. 296–373) argued for the central place of the concept of *Logos* in Christian theology: 'by the direction, providence, and ordering of the *Logos*, the creation [is] illumined and enabled to abide always securely' (*Against the Heathen*).

St Augustine (354–430) believed that Plato had already intuited the truth of the pre-existing *Logos* referred to in John's Gospel. In 'certain books of the Platonists … I read, not indeed in the very words, but to the very same purpose … that In the beginning was the Word, and the Word was with God, and the Word was God … But that the Word was made flesh, and dwelt among us, I read not there … That He emptied Himself, taking the form of a servant … and became obedient unto death, and that the death of the cross ... those books have not' (*Confessions*, Book 7).

Martin Heidegger (1889–1976): an existentialist philosopher who argued that the Christian–Platonic conception of the *Logos* had been a philosophical mistake. Heidegger said that the emphasis upon truth as a rational *Logos* meant that Western culture had overlooked the basic question of human existence. Instead of allowing the truth of existence to show itself, we have tried to analyse 'truth' in the abstract. If we want to understand the *Logos* correctly, said Heidegger, we need to return to Heraclitus' conception of the *Logos* as the 'gathering' and 'calling' of something more fundamental – namely, 'Being'.

Karl Barth (1886–1968) put the concept of the Word of God at the centre of his theology. The Word takes three forms: (i) the incarnate *Logos*; (ii) the written Word of Scripture; (iii) the Word of God as preached by the Church.

Justin Martyr (100?–165?) pointed out that some ancient Greek thinkers – in particular, the pre-Socratic philosopher Heraclitus – had argued that the *Logos* 'governs all things'. Justin saw Heraclitus as a Christian before Christ.

The Stoics (third century BC) used the term *Logos* for the creative force in the cosmos.

IDEAS

The Alogi: a second-century sect who, among other things, rejected the *Logos* theology in John's Gospel.

Logos spermatikos: the concept of the 'seminal Word' referred to by the Stoics and developed by Justin Martyr.

Logotherapy: a form of psychotherapy developed by Viktor Frankl (1905–97), a psychotherapist who regarded the desire for meaning as the primary force in human nature.

Logocentrism: a term coined by Jacques Derrida to describe the restrictive and controlling pattern of Western thinking, which operates in terms of fixed structures and hierarchies of meaning.

Alexandrian theology: a second-century school of *Logos*-theology associated with Clement of Alexandria, Origen and Athanasius. Clement was a philosopher-theologian who regarded classic Greek philosophy as a valuable grounding for Christian theology.

The Cosmic Christ: the idea (associated with Pierre Teilhard de

Chardin, but with a heritage going back to the *Logos*-theology of the Church Fathers) of Christ as the incarnate meaning and purpose of the cosmos.

BOOKS

Wolfhart Pannenberg, *Jesus: God and Man* (Westminster/John Knox Press, 1982)

Henny Fiska Hägg, *Clement of Alexandria and the Beginnings of Christian Apophaticism* (OUP, 2006)

Miracles

Things done by God that break the known laws of nature.

The word 'miracle' derives from the Latin *miraculum*, meaning 'something wonderful'. In the religious sense, a miracle is an act of divine intervention. Belief in miracles has been an important part of Christian theology since the earliest times. Jesus' miracles were evidence of his divine status and the miracles of the apostles were signs of their authority. The Roman Catholic Church still regards miracles as evidence of sainthood.

In the modern period, however, the question of whether miracles are possible has been bitterly disputed, with liberal theologians abandoning all sense of a supernatural religion. David Hume's devastating attack on miracles in his essay 'Of Miracles' has attained an iconic status in modern philosophy. Hume's critique became symbolic of the entire Enlightenment rejection of religion. By challenging the reality of miracles, Hume was aiming to challenge the credibility of any kind of supernatural activity or existence. Hume says that his argument against miracles will be 'an everlasting check to all kinds of superstitious delusion'. The rejection of miracles implied the rejection of everything supernatural, all revelation and all prophecy. Hume said that without belief in miracles, it was unreasonable to have faith in the Christian religion.

The question of miracles was the subject of much debate in the early eighteenth century, and Hume's essay emerged in the midst of these controversies. The debate began with the Deists, who believed that God had established the world as a well-ordered system with rational laws. It would be irrational for God to intervene to change his own divine plan: a miracle would be an admission by God that his general laws had been inadequate, and God cannot logically be inadequate. The Deists also argued that the word 'miracle' is merely a label used for any strange thing that has not yet been explained by science.

The Deist case is appealing, but it depends upon the presumption that the world really is a machine operating according to regular laws that we can fully understand. Miracles could simply be unusual instances of God's activity which follow a rationality we cannot understand.

Hume's argument against miracles was simple and effective, and ran like this: We only know about the miracles in Scripture from the testimony of others. But it is only reasonable to accept the testimony of others as true, when it fits with our own experience. Since we have no experience of walking on water, or resurrections, it is not reasonable to take the testimony of others on these matters as true.

Critics of Hume say that his argument depends upon the improbability of miracles. If miracles are improbable, then it is not reasonable to give credence to reports of miracles. However, the occasional occurrence of the improbable is probable. It may be improbable that I will win the national lottery three times in a row, but it is possible. Walking on water may be even more improbable, but it cannot be ruled out altogether. Hume's argument shows that belief in miracles is unreasonable, but it does not show that miracles themselves are impossible.

Hume's concluding point is that belief in miracles must be an act of faith rather than reason. This is surely correct. Even if we accept the testimony of someone who claims to have seen a vision of the Virgin Mary, it requires an act of faith to believe that this vision was given by God.

Very few people now truly believe in the power of miracles. Sick people take themselves to the doctor and only start praying in desperation for miracles when science has failed. Anyone who truly believed in God's power to intervene would presumably start praying straight away and save their bus fare to the hospital.

THINKERS

Elizabeth Anscombe (1919–2001), in a public lecture, demolished C. S. Lewis' argument that miracles prove the existence of God. Lewis was, allegedly, deeply humiliated by the experience.

St Augustine (354–430) argued in *The City of God* that miracles do not violate the laws of nature, but only our understanding of nature. God makes miracles possible within nature, but his purposes are too hidden for us to understand.

Samuel Clarke (1675–1729) argued against the Deists in *A Discourse concerning the Unchangeable Obligations of Natural Religion and the Truth of Christian Revelation* (1705), saying that a miracle is not a violation of natural laws, but simply an unusual instance of God's rational activity.

William Lane Craig (1949–) argues that miracles should not be ruled out as logically impossible, but should be judged on the empirical evidence in each individual case.

Thomas Hobbes (1588–1679) rejected supernatural explanations in favour of a scientific understanding: 'Thence it is that ignorant and superstitious men make great wonders of those works which other men, knowing to proceed from nature (which is not the immediate, but the ordinary work of God), admire not at all' (*Leviathan*).

C. S. Lewis (1898–1963) argued in his book *Miracles* that it is rational to believe in God and supernatural phenomena.

Hermann Reimarus (1694–1758): a German Deist who argued that, since true religion is reached by the exercise of reason, belief in miracles cannot be part of a true religion. It would be irrational to suppose that God would transgress his own natural laws.

Baruch de Spinoza (1632–77) ruled out belief in miracles on principle, arguing that God would have no need to alter his plan for nature. Belief in miracles happens out of ignorance of the natural causes of things.

François Voltaire (1694–1778) argued, with the Deists, that it would be 'the most absurd of all extravagances to imagine that the infinite Supreme Being would on behalf of three or four hundred emmets on this little atom of mud derange the operation of the vast machinery that moves the universe' ('Miracles' in the *Philosophical Dictionary*).

Thomas Woolston (1669–1733) argued in his *Discourses on the Miracles of our Saviour* that the miracles of Jesus, including the resurrection, should be read as allegories.

IDEAS

Coincidence: this is different from a miracle, even if it is startling. A miracle must involve the direct action of God. So turning up late for a bus that crashes is fortunate, but not a miracle, unless God intervened in some supernatural way to stop you boarding the bus.

Littlewood's Law: a ludicrous but entertaining theory formulated by John Littlewood (1885–1977), that a miracle (defined as a one-in-a-million event) will happen to someone in the world at least once every month.

Providence: God's ongoing activity in nature and history. So the provision of harvests each year is providential rather than miraculous.

BOOKS

Ian Ramsey (ed.), *The Reasonableness of Christianity, and a Discourse of Miracles* (Stanford University Press, 1958)

Mysticism

The belief that God can be encountered directly through prayer and other spiritual disciplines.

The word 'mysticism' derives from the Greek term *mysterion*, meaning 'secret'. In the New Testament the word *mysterion* is used to describe the hidden meaning of the cosmos: the parables of Jesus are described as *mysterion*, and St Paul speaks about the *mysterion* as 'the secret and hidden wisdom of God, which God decreed before the ages for our glorification' (1 Cor. 2:7).

Now the word 'mysticism' is used in a catch-all sense to indicate any approach to religious life and theology that tries to access dimensions of experience normally concealed in everyday life. We may speak of mysticism in the experience of music, art, literature, philosophy, meditation and nature. Mystical experiences may or may not be theistic, may or may not involve a direct divine encounter, and may occur in a range of religious and non-religious individuals. Some mystical experiences are rooted in a specific religious tradition, and others point to a universal and eternal dimension beyond religion.

When we try to define mystical experience, we soon find that it resists easy description. William James (in his *Varieties of Religious Experience*) argued that 'ineffability' is the defining characteristic of mystical religion, meaning that it transcends language.

The mystical approach to God is also normally distinguished from rational theology. Mysticism transcends ordinary knowledge of God and theological reasoning: the mystic encounters the essence of the reality of God, beyond mere ideas about him. Thus the mystic may often speak about his/her experience in metaphors, paradoxes and apparent impossibilities.

Mystical experience is normally seen as transcending or transfiguring ordinary sense experience. The mystic may, for example, claim to experience something mystical in seeing a beautiful sunset, but the mystical content of this experience is not publicly verifiable, and someone else seeing exactly the same event may not perceive it as having any religious content.

There are many examples of mystical experience in the Bible. Moses is recorded as having mystical experiences of God, and the prophets received visions from God. Jesus' disciples saw him strangely 'transfigured' in the company of Elijah and Moses. And St Paul was converted in a mystical encounter with Jesus.

Mystical experience has always been an important dimension of Christian experience and theology. The influence of Plato and Plotinus on the Christian mystical tradition has been very significant. Plato emphasised the role of love and desire, and saw the movement towards the divine as a dialectical process of reasoning guided by an inner love of truth. Plotinus saw the ascent towards God (or 'the One') as a natural movement of God's creative energy back to himself. God emanates himself out into the created order, and this emanation draws back to him like a tidal current. Through spiritual friendship (the so-called 'Platonic friendship') and intellectual reflection, the inner spiritual person may attain a sense of unity with God. (See 'Negative Theology'.)

The principal difficulty of all mysticism is that it remains personal to the individual. If mystical experience is 'ineffable', then it cannot be communicated directly to others. If mysticism is non-rational, or supra-rational, then it cannot easily be explained to others. And if it transcends the ordinary public senses, then it cannot be shown to others. This gives mysticism a strongly private character.

It is for this reason, among others, that mysticism has been so congenial to our individualistic, post-modern culture in which New Age religions have flourished on talk of ineffable, personalised truth and transcendent experiences.

The most vital strain of Christian mysticism today is arguably to be found in the music of composers such as Olivier Messiaen, Henryk Górecki, Arvo Pärt and John Tavener. This new Christian mystical music is enjoying considerable popularity: recordings of Górecki's *Third Symphony* have sold on a scale normally reserved for pop musicians, and Tavener's music was used at the funeral of Princess Diana.

THINKERS

St Augustine (354–422) records in Book 9 of the *Confessions* that he had a mystical vision in prayerful contemplation with his mother in Ostia: 'my mother and I ... were talking alone together and our conversation was serene and joyful ... As the flame of love burned stronger in us and raised us higher towards the eternal God ... At length we came to our own souls and passed beyond them to that place of everlasting plenty, where you feed Israel for ever with the food of truth.'

Jakob Böhme (1575–1624): a seventeenth-century shoemaker who saw direct affinity between the human soul and the reality of God: 'I did not climb up into the Godhead, neither can so mean a man as I am do it; but the Godhead climbed up in me, and revealed such to me out of his Love' (*Aurora*).

Denys (or Dionysius) the Areopagite (c. 500) argued in *The Mystical Theology* that knowledge of God comes from mystical practice.

Marsilio Ficino (1433–99): a classic 'Renaissance man' (scholar, doctor, musician, priest) who drew upon the writings of Plato and Plotinus to develop a *pia philosophia* (sacred philosophy) structured around the immortality of the human soul and its ascent towards God: 'There are three principal steps in Platonic contemplation. The first ascends from the body through the soul to God, the second abides still in God and the third descends to the soul and the body.'

Henryk Górecki (1933–): an avant-garde Polish Catholic composer who uses liturgical and other sources to create a sacred, mystical sound-scape.

Olivier Messiaen (1908–92): a French Catholic composer who explored the relationship between time and eternity in his music.

Rudolf Otto (1869–1937) wrote a classic work, *The Idea of the Holy*, in which he argues that religion is founded on 'non-rational, non-sensory experience' of something numinous beyond the self. The numinous is a *mysterium tremendum*, something both mysterious and terrifying.

Arvo Pärt (1935–): an Estonian composer who developed the technique of 'tintinnabulation' or building up sound from simple components, producing a unique style of Christian mystical music.

John Tavener (1944–): a Greek Orthodox composer who strives to communicate the mystical in his minimalist music.

IDEAS

Asceticism: the practice of seeking religious insight by denying oneself earthly comforts.

The numinous: a word indicating the dimension of the sacred and spiritual. (The word 'numinous' was used by Kant in a specific philosophic sense to refer to 'things in themselves' beyond our perception of them.)

Ladder spirituality has been a staple of Christian mysticism. Jacob's ladder combined with Plato's ideas about the ascent of the soul planted a powerful image in Christian theology: the picture of prayer as a mystical ascent towards God. Notable examples of this tradition have been St John Climicus' *The Ladder of Divine Ascent* and Walter Hilton's *The Ladder of Perfection*. The ladder of spiritual ascent is contrasted by Origen with the 'wheel' of the imagination, which merely recycles human thoughts.

BOOKS

Andrew Louth, *The Origins of the Christian Mystical Tradition* (OUP, 2007)

William Alston, *Perceiving God: The Epistemology of Religious Experience* (Cornell University Press, 1991)

Myth

A form of sacred story that illuminates the truth of the human condition.

The ancient myths were sacred stories involving the gods (and possibly humans) and were set in a cosmological landscape outside recognisable history. But we now regard a myth as any story which takes on a sacred or cultic function for a particular culture or community.

Since the Enlightenment, mythic thinking has increasingly been regarded as the opposite of scientific thinking about facts and reality. It became fashionable in the modern period, for example, to demythologise the Gospels to reveal the 'factual' Jesus beneath the various mythic stories about him. (See 'Biblical Criticism'.) The demythologisers rather missed the point that the myths about Jesus were intended to reveal the truth about him and cannot be disentangled from the more historically grounded parts of the Gospel narratives. Jesus cannot be treated as an historical figure separate from his mythic identity – indeed, Jesus' mythic identity is arguably more significant than the factual story of his life. The facts give us the details, but the myth tells us Jesus' significance and sacred meaning.

This point was made very well by C. S. Lewis who, with his friend J. R. R. Tolkien, became fascinated by the mythic dimension to the Christian story:

> The heart of Christianity is a myth which is also a fact. The old myth of the Dying God, *without ceasing to be myth*, comes down from the heaven of legend and imagination to the earth of history ... By becoming fact it does not cease to be myth: ... We must not be ashamed of the mythical radiance resting on

our theology. We must not be nervous about 'parallels' and 'pagan Christs': they *ought* to be there – it would be a stumbling block if they weren't. We must not, in false spirituality, withhold our imaginative welcome. If God chooses to be mythopoeic – and is not the sky itself a myth – shall we refuse to be *mythopathic*?

> (C. S. Lewis, 'Myth Became Fact', in *God in the Dock*)

The contrast between 'myth' and 'history' is unhelpful because the two are closely connected: histories and myths both tell stories, and most historians are shown in retrospect to be in the grip of the mythic structures of their age. Even factually truthful histories can take on a mythic status and function as cultural narratives that embody spiritual or moral meanings. This is arguably true for the history of the Holocaust, which now has (in addition to its factuality) a mythic status as a sacred story for our times. A myth arises when the events and protagonists in a story/history take on a religious or cosmic significance.

Adorno and Horkheimer argued in *The Dialectic of Enlightenment* that modern Western culture had been fuelled by an attempt to eliminate 'primitive' mythic ideas from human thinking and replace them with a more 'enlightened' and scientific consciousness. But, they argued, the idea of 'enlightenment' is itself just another myth: the illusion that humans can dispense with mythic narratives.

The same point has been made by others. Mircea Eliade has argued that modern people are as conditioned by myths as their 'primitive' forebears. But our modern mythology is a poor substitute for the pre-modern myths that evoked a sense of the sacred which Eliade believed to be fundamental to human self-understanding. Modern myths – such as the *Star Wars* myth of a Manichaean universe contested by opposing light and dark forces – are now driven by the media rather than organised religion.

THINKERS

Aristotle (384–322 BC) contrasted *mythos* and story-telling with *logos* and rational thinking.

Ernst Cassirer (1874–1945): a Jewish philosopher who saw humans as 'symbolic animals' who fashion 'symbolic forms', including myths: 'language, myth, art, and science ... function organically together in the constitution of spiritual reality.'

Mircea Eliade (1907–86): a Romanian Christian influenced by Jung, who argued that human beings have a natural and primary need for sacred myths.

James George Frazer (1854–1941): author of *The Golden Bough*, a classic study of religious myth, which argued that Jesus was just one example of a general myth of the 'dying God'.

Carl Jung (1875–1961) explored the mythic content of the unconscious and related it to fundamental and universal aspects of mythic thinking in culture: 'the fund of unconscious images which fatally confuse the mental patient ... is also the matrix of a mythopoeic imagination which has vanished from our rational age.'

Claude Lévi-Strauss (1908–) analysed the basic structure of myths in terms of 'binary oppositions' – in particular, the contrast between 'nature' and 'culture'. Myths are complex elaborations of the tensions between opposites. Lévi Strauss popularised the analysis of modern culture in terms of its mythological structures.

J. R. R. Tolkien (1892–1973) believed that the Christian truths were best expressed in stories, principally the narrative of the Gospel, which he saw as 'the greatest story of all'. But he felt that the language of doctrine was too restricted and thin to gather up the rich and complex truth of Christianity. So Tolkien committed himself to mythopoesis: the construction of new myths to re-express the essence of the Christian message – for example, *The Lord of the Rings*.

IDEAS

Archteype: a primitive image, motif or character in a myth or narrative.

Demytholgisation: see 'Biblical Criticism'.

Legend: a traditional story belonging to the history or pre-history of a culture.

Mythopoesis: the construction of myths.

BOOKS

Laurence Coupe, *Myth* (Routledge, 1997)

Leszek Kolakowski, *The Presence of Myth* (University of Chicago Press, 1988)

Rudolf Bultmann, 'New Testament and Mythology', and Karl Jaspers, 'Myth and Religion', both in *Kerygma and Myth* (SPCK, 1972)

Narrative Theology

An approach to theology that sees stories as the basic structure of theological knowledge.

Narrative theology is often seen as a late-twentieth-century development, and there has certainly been considerable interest in the theory of narrative in recent decades. However, the roots of narrative theology can be traced much further back into Christian tradition.

The Jewish Scriptures valued the practice of story-telling and history-telling as a form of theology. The Jewish confession of faith was not a creed but a story: 'You shall make a response before the Lord: "My father was a wandering Aramean, he went down into Egypt and sojourned there ..."' (Deut. 26:5). The practice of story-telling was prominent in Jesus' use of parables; and the first Christians treasured the stories of Jesus' life and teaching as their primary theological asset.

Although the influence of Greek philosophy made early Christian theology increasingly abstract, a narrative theological approach remained a powerful dimension in theology. St Augustine's autobiography, the *Confessions*, is a unique example of theological narrative, but stories feature widely as the medium for special revelations: Jerome, Gregory of Nyssa, Gregory of Naziansus and Perpetua all had narrative dream-visions by which they set great store.

Much later in the history of the Church, the case for narrative theology was argued eloquently by John Bunyan in the verse preface to his *Pilgrim's Progress*:

> May I not write in such a style as this?
> In such a method too, and yet not miss
> Mine end, thy good? Why may it not be done?

> By metaphors I speak; was not God's laws,
> His Gospel-laws in olden time held forth
> By types, shadows and metaphors?

The twentieth-century interest in narrative theology coincided with the general interest in theological language that was inspired by the thinking of Ludwig Wittgenstein, Martin Heidegger, Ferdinand de Saussure and others. There was a growing consensus, which crossed conservative and liberal lines, that a consideration of language was not just one subject among others, but the most important area of theology. This is because all our theological thinking takes place in language.

The central insight of narrative theology was the idea that both life and language are structured as stories, making narrative our primary means of self-understanding. This would mean – as George Lindbeck and others have suggested – that Christian doctrine must be understood in terms of linguistic structures.

This marked a significant move away from the established idea that narrative and myth were secondary to reason. Narrative theology suggested that stories were a legitimate, and perhaps superior, method of reasoning. In this way, narrative theology appeared to challenge the liberal–Enlightenment confidence in human rationality.

In its conservative form (expressed by Stanley Hauerwas and John Milbank, for example), narrative theology argues that Christianity is in essence a living story. The Christian task is to live within this narrative and re-narrate the story for the world.

Liberals (such as David Tracy, for example) question whether there is just one narrative that holds together all the disparate strands of the Christian revelation. The Bible itself contains multiple narratives and the history of the Church shows that the Christian story comes in many versions. For liberals, narrative theology shows that the Christian revelation is not a 'master narrative' but contains multiple narrative possibilities.

THINKERS

John Dominic Crossan (1934–) has emphasised the importance of subversive parables in Jesus' theology.

Hans Frei (1922–88): a pioneering theologian of narrative who established the so-called New Yale School, which also included George Lindbeck.

C. S. Lewis (1898–1963) agreed with J. R. R. Tolkien and the other so-called 'Inklings' (a literary society interested in imaginative fiction) that 'the heart of Christianity is a myth which is also a fact.' (See 'Myth'.)

George Lindbeck (1923–) used the linguistic philosophy of Wittgenstein to offer a cultural-linguistic understanding of doctrine. (See 'Doctrine'.)

George MacDonald (1824–1905): a Christian fantasy writer who argued in *Phantastes* (1858) that the imagination is the true medium of theological thinking.

Plato (427–347 BC) suggested that the best that philosophy could hope for was to tell 'likely stories'.

Paul Ricoeur (1913–2005): a French theologian and philosopher who argued in *Time and Narrative* that life must be understood as story/history.

Charles Williams (1886–1945): a novelist who used fiction to explore theology and spirituality. He was a major influence on C. S. Lewis.

IDEAS

The Dream of the Rood (author unknown): a ninth-century Anglo-Saxon narrative about a vision of the cross. It is the oldest example in English of a genre of imaginative Christian narrative which continues in later mystical poems such as *Pearl*, *Patience* and *Sir Gawain and the Green Knight*.

The New Yale School, founded by Hans Frei and sometimes called 'post-liberalism', argued for the importance of language and narrative in orthodox theology.

Structuralism: an approach to narrative, used notably by Roland Barthes and Algirdas Greimas, which reduced the essence of stories to basic diagrammatic structures.

The Christian Mythos: the term used by John Milbank to describe the defining narrative of Christendom.

Narratology: the study of narrative.

Mythopoesis ('the making of myths'): a concept put forward by J. R. R. Tolkien, who believed that Christian truth is best expressed in stories – principally the narrative of the Gospel, which he saw as 'the greatest story of all'.

BOOKS

Don Cupitt, *What is a Story?* (SCM, 1991)
Stanley Hauerwas and L. Gregory Jones (eds.), *Why Narrative? Readings in Narrative Theology* (Wipf & Stock, 1997)

Natural Theology

A form of theology that takes its knowledge of God from nature rather than from revelation.

St Thomas Aquinas was the first to make the distinction between 'natural theology' and 'revealed theology'. 'Natural theology' assumes that we can understand something of God using our natural faculties of reason and ordinary experience. 'Revealed theology' assumes that our knowledge of God must come through special channels of divine revelation, such as the Bible or supernatural experiences.

Natural theology predates Christianity and can be found, for example, in Aristotle, who believed that the natural world is a rational system of causes and effects. God, for Aristotle, is 'the first cause' or 'unmoved mover'. Thomas Aquinas built upon Aristotle's philosophy to develop his own natural theology. Aquinas argued that there is an 'analogy of being' (*analogia entis*) between God and his creation. Although infinitely inferior to God, the created world is still God's work, and consequently we can draw an analogy between what we see in nature and the reality of God.

Natural theology assumes, first, that God has created a rational, purposeful and ordered world; and secondly, that God has given us the faculties of perception and reason with which to appreciate the design of his creation. This way of thinking became popular in the eighteenth and early nineteenth centuries when natural science appeared to be proving natural theology right by revealing the basic laws of the universe.

The most famous case for natural theology was offered by William Paley, who devised the so-called 'Watchmaker Argument'. If we found a watch on the ground, we would assume the existence of a watchmaker; similarly, when we see the design of the world, we assume the existence of a creator God.

Natural theology suffered a crippling blow from David Hume, who delivered a withering attack on it in his *Dialogues Concerning Natural Religion*. Hume's main point was that while we know from experience that watches have watchmakers, we cannot know from experience that worlds have creators. We do not know how worlds are generated, and it is not logical to assume that they are made in the same fashion as human artefacts.

Hume's arguments – and others against natural theology – have to be taken seriously. But some kind of natural theology is essential if we are to reconcile theological and scientific knowledge. If our reason and experience can tell us nothing about God, then science – whose building-blocks are reason and experience – can contribute nothing to theology. But the kind of natural theology we need is not Paley's naïve concept of design (currently being revived by the Intelligent Design lobby) but a theology that works to reconcile the real achievements of science with the revealed insights of theology.

THINKERS

Aristotle (384–322 BC) argued that everything in the natural world has a teleological purpose: 'Nature does nothing in vain.'

St Augustine (354–430) first used the term 'natural theology' to describe the theological reflections of the pre-Christian classical philosophers, who could not benefit from the revelation of God in Jesus Christ.

Karl Barth (1886–1968) argued that all knowledge of God arises from God's self-revelation. (See 'Analogy of faith'.)

Charles Darwin (1809–82): although he admired William Paley's design argument as a young man, his own theory of evolution contradicted Paley's view that the natural world had been 'designed' by God.

Stanley Hauerwas (1940–) has argued strongly that proper natural religion must be based upon revealed religion, because an investigation of the natural world that is not informed by God must be in error. Thus Hauerwas reckons Karl Barth, of all people, to be the best kind of natural theologian!

Richard Hooker (1554–1600) argued the very Anglican view that we need both revealed and natural theology: 'Nature and Scripture do serve in such full sort that they both jointly and not severally either of them be so complete that unto everlasting felicity we need not the knowledge of anything more than these two may easily furnish.'

William James (1842–1910), in *The Varieties of Religious Experience*, objected that the God of natural theology 'must be a God of universal laws exclusively, a God who does a wholesale, not a retail business. He cannot accommodate his processes to the convenience of individuals ... [whose] destinies weigh nothing and determine nothing in the world's irremediable currents of events.'

John Ray (1628–1705) argued that God could be understood by studying his creation: 'There is ... no occupation more worthy and delightful than to contemplate the beauteous works of nature and honour the infinite wisdom and goodness of God.'

William Paley (1743–1805), in his *Natural Theology, or Evidences of the Existence and Attributes of the Deity* (1802), compared nature to a watch found on the ground: 'When we come to inspect the watch, we perceive ... that its several parts are framed and put together for a purpose ... the inference we think is inevitable, that the watch must have had a maker.'

St Paul (3–65) argued at the Areopagus in Athens that the Athenians had reached an understanding of an 'unknown God' without any revealed knowledge of God.

IDEAS

Analogia entis: the doctrine, associated with Thomas Aquinas, that God can be known by analogy with his creation.

The Bridgewater Treatises: eight books 'on the Power, Wisdom and Goodness of God as manifested in the Creation', commissioned by Revd Francis Henry Egerton, the Earl of Bridgewater, in the early nineteenth century.

The Deists relied exclusively on natural theology, on the grounds that the being and attributes of God are revealed perfectly in the workings of the natural world.

Intelligent Design: a form of the design argument revived by fundamentalist Christians in the early twenty-first century. The argument suffers from all the weaknesses of the eighteenth-century arguments from design.

Revealed theology: theology that assumes that all knowledge of God must come from special divine revelation, as it says in the hymn: 'Judge not the Lord by feeble sense'.

BOOKS

James Barr, *Biblical Faith and Natural Theology* (OUP, 1995)

Stanley Hauerwas, *With the Grain of the Universe: The Church's Witness and Natural Theology* (Brazos Press, 2001)

Alister McGrath, *The Order of Things: Explorations in Scientific Theology* (Blackwell, 2006)

Negative Theology

A theology that speaks of God by saying what he is not.

Negative theology, or the *via negativa* (negative way), tries to describe God either in negative statements or by avoiding speaking directly about God. Negative theology is particularly important in Eastern Orthodox Christianity and in the Christian mystical tradition.

The presupposition of negative theology is that human thoughts and languages are by their nature incapable of describing divine reality. To speak positively of God, by saying God is X or Y, would be both presumptuous and untruthful. The only way to avoid this mistake is to find a way of talking about God by *not talking about him*.

We could think of negative theology through the analogy of sculpture. The sculptor cuts away at a block of stone, removing unwanted material until the design is revealed. As the sculptor shapes the figure by subtraction, so negative theology reveals God by showing what he is not.

The biblical roots of negative theology lie in the sermons against idolatry that we find in the Old Testament prophets, such as Deutero-Isaiah, who insists that the 'living God' is too vast for any human portrayal: 'To whom can you compare God? What image can you contrive of him?' (Isa. 40:18).

The philosophical origins of negative theology lie in Platonism and neo-Platonism. Plato had declared that the highest reality (the Good) was 'beyond being'. The neo-Platonist thinker Plotinus, for example, describes God (or 'the One') as formless, unmeasurable and infinite. Although we can make a contemplative journey towards God, we must in the end relinquish all attempts at understanding in order to reach out to God in his pure one-ness. This final abandonment to God is what Plotinus called 'the flight of the alone to the alone'.

A weak form of negative theology – that is to say, the belief that God transcends human thoughts and words – has always been implicit in Christian thinking, and most theologians would argue for the value of negative theology alongside positive theology. Some mystical theologians, however, have believed that positive theology is impossible, and that the negative path is the only road that theologians should take. This reaches an extreme form in Meister Eckhart's refusal to say even that God exists and Angelus Silesius' talk about the 'nothingness' of God. Recently, there has been a revival of interest in the *via negativa* among some post-modern theologians (for example, Mark C. Taylor, Kevin Hart and John Caputo).

The principal objection to a wholly negative theology is that we cannot make negative judgements about God without first having some positive knowledge of him. The statement, 'God is not evil' presumes some positive understanding that God is good. The sculptor can only chip off unwanted stone because he knows the shape that he wants to emerge underneath.

Negative theology has also had an impact on modern secular philosophy. Theodor Adorno's *Negative Dialectics* (1973) is an example. Adorno thought that positive truth claims lead to totalitarianism and fascism, and advocated 'a negation of negation that will not become a positing ... It lies in the definition of negative dialectics that it will not come to rest in itself as if it were total. This is its form of hope' (*Negative Dialectics*).

The legacy of negative theology can also be seen in some post-modern artists. The sparse canvases of Barnett Newman's *Stations of the Cross* have no figures of Christ, just abstract lines leaving the viewer to deduce God (or not) from their theological emptiness. Mark Rothko's brooding panes of dark colour are another example of a secular negative theology. Rothko evokes a sense of the mystical without ever describing it, which is why his paintings can work in a multi-religious 'spiritual environment' like The Rothko Chapel (Houston, Texas). Similarly, Samuel Beckett's *Waiting for Godot* can be read in the light of negative theology as an attempt to speak about the divine through its absence.

THINKERS

St Thomas Aquinas argued that negative theology was a necessary preliminary to any positive theology.

Denys (or Dionysius) the Areopagite – also called Pseudo-Dionysius (c. 500) – argued in his *Mystical Theology* that, although we can contemplate God in a symbolic way through metaphors and names, God himself is wholly beyond our ability to comprehend.

Petru Dumitriu (1924–2002): a Romanian writer who argued, in *To The Unknown God* (1979), that God is most real in silence and absence.

Johannes ('Meister') Eckhart (c. 1260–1327/8) argued that negative theology must go so far as declaring God to be non-existent. This was not an atheistic statement, rather a refusal to define God by human concepts of 'existence'. Near the end of his life he was tried as a heretic by Pope John XXII.

St John of the Cross (1542–91) wrote mystical theology and poetry, believing that the closer we get to God, the less we comprehend: 'In my soul I felt, revealing,/ A sense that, though its sense was naught,/ Transcended knowledge with my thought' (from 'Verses written after an ecstasy of high exaltation').

St Paul (3–65) tells in Acts 17 of seeing an altar dedicated to 'the unknown God' – an example of negative theological description. Paul argued that 'the unknown God' is in fact 'known' in the form of the Christian God, 'in whom we live and move and have our being'.

Angelus Silesius/Johannes Scheffer (1624–77) argued for an extreme negative theology in *The Cherubic Wanderer*, saying that

'God is sheer nothingness ... To become nothing is to become God.'

Gregory of Nyssa (c. 335–c. 394) argued that God's infinity necessarily makes him unknowable.

Plato (427–347 BC) described 'the Good' (or the highest reality) as 'beyond being' – *epekeina tes ousias* (*The Republic*, 508b) – and therefore beyond the reach of thought and language.

Plotinus (205–70) believed that we must abandon ourselves to God in contemplation rather than trying to understand him.

Proclus (412–85) argued in *The Elements of Theology* that 'the gods are superessential, and subsist prior to beings; they cannot be apprehended by opinion, science or discursive reason, or by intelligence' (Proposition 123).

The Cloud of Unknowing, an anonymous fourteenth-century spiritual book, says that 'of God Himself no man can think'. 'Your intense need to understand will ... undermine your quest [to find God]. It will replace the darkness which you have pierced ... with clear images of something which, however good, however beautiful, however Godlike, is not God.'

IDEAS

Apophatic theology: another term for negative theology, and the opposite of kataphatic (or positive) theology.

Aufhebung: a concept in Hegel's philosophy which means 'negating in order to move forward'.

The Dark Night of the Soul: a spiritual discipline, described by St John of the Cross, that uses the absence of knowledge and the senses as a 'secret ladder' to reach God.

'Negative capability': a term used by John Keats to describe the state 'when man is capable of being in uncertainties, Mysteries, doubts, without any irritable reaching after fact and reason.'

Otherness of God: the idea that God is essentially strange to us.

BOOKS

Denys Turner and Oliver Davies (eds.), *Silence and the Word: Negative Theology and Incarnation* (CUP, 2002)

Philosophy of Religion

The philosophical study of the truth claims, presuppositions and arguments of religion.

The philosophy of religion is the philosophical analysis of religious claims to truth. Unlike general theology, or 'philosophical theology' (see below), the philosophy of religion is not committed to any particular theological or religious view. Rather, it subjects all theological views to interrogation and critique.

At the centre of the philosophy of religion has been the question of whether it is reasonable to believe in God, and indeed, what kind of God it is reasonable to believe in. Other important issues are the problem of evil, miracles, life after death and the nature of religious language.

The last of these has come to dominate contemporary philosophy of religion. Since all our philosophical reasoning must take place in language, the question of the status of that language is absolutely crucial. Some recent philosophers of religion, strongly influenced by Wittgenstein and post-structuralist language theory, regard all linguistic meaning as a social construct. This implies that the meaning of the word 'God' is just an agreed convention. Other philosophers of religion have argued against this, saying that religious language is only meaningful if it can be shown to refer to objective realities.

How the philosophy of religion is practised depends upon what one means by 'philosophy'. The most common definition is that philosophy is a form of questioning and enquiry. The method used by Socrates – as we see from Plato's depiction of him – was a process of questioning the views of others. By asking the right questions, Socrates tried to eliminate false arguments and reveal the truth. Aristotle saw philosophy in more analytical terms as 'inquiry' (*historia*). The philosopher should conduct a careful analysis of the 'reputable opinions' (*endoxa*) on the subject. From this the philosopher draws up a list of problems (*aporia*) that must be worked through in order to reach the truth of the matter.

R. G. Collingwood in the twentieth century helpfully described philosophy as 'the science of absolute presuppositions' (*Essays on*

Metaphysics), meaning that philosophy should look beneath the surface of thought to question the fundamental assumptions upon which our thinking is based.

But if philosophy is just relentless questioning, enquiry and inter-rogation, where is its commitment to truth? The word 'philosophy' means literally 'the love of wisdom', which implies that questioning is the *method* of philosophy rather than its *identity*. In Book 6 of *The Republic* Plato says that the 'philosophic nature' must be a love for the truth. So philosophical questioning must be motivated by a commit-ment to the truth (however complex, ungraspable or apparently impossible). Without this love of truth, says Plato, philosophy becomes the province of 'useless cranks'.

The philosophy or religion, then, should subject religious claims and presuppositions to rigorous examination, but should do so with a concern to uncover the truth. A purely critical philosophy of religion would be vulnerable itself to the philosophical questioning of its own motivation and purposes.

An objection that can be made to all philosophy of religion is that theology cannot, by definition, be verified or falsified by human reason. Karl Barth, for example, argued that the attempt to judge theology by reason is irrelevant to faith. 'God is love' is a revealed truth which no amount of human reasoning can change.

But a religion that is not subjected to rigorous questioning is at risk of deluding itself. Philosophy of religion protects religion against error and should be an integral part of theological practice. To function properly, philosophy of religion must be given an absolutely free hand to question and investigate any aspect of religious reason-ing or any claim to truth. When religions claim that they are too sacred to be questioned, we can be sure that they have degenerated into fundamentalism.

THINKERS

Thomas Aquinas (1225–74) argued that philosophy and theology have distinct perspectives: 'The believer and the philosopher con-sider creatures differently. The philosopher considers what belongs to their proper natures, while the believer considers only what is true of creatures insofar as they are related to God, for example, that they are created by God and are subject to him, and the like' (*Summa Contra Gentiles*).

St Augustine (354–430) noted the remarkable similarity between Plato's philosophy and elements of Christian theology: 'with the change of a few words and opinions many Platonists have become Christians' (*On True Religion*). This illustrated, for Augustine, the coherence of faith and reason/philosophy.

Rudolf Carnap (1891–1970) was typical of the logical positivists in arguing that the role of philosophy is to demonstrate the inadequacy of all theological claims, which he regarded as 'metaphysical pseudostatements'.

Martin Heidegger (1889–1976) called faith 'the mortal enemy' of philosophy (*Phenomenology and Theology*) because religion has pre-packed answers to the meaning of human existence, and therefore does not engage in philosophical analysis of our existential condition: 'there can be no such thing as a Christian philosophy; that is an absolute "square circle".' Elsewhere Heidegger comments that 'the Christian experience is so completely different that it does not need to enter into competition with philosophy.'

Jean-Luc Marion (1946–) argued in *God Without Being* that philosophy and theology operate in different domains.

St Paul (3–65) held discussions with 'certain Epicurean and Stoic philosophers' at the Areopagus in Athens (Acts 17:18). He argued that the God reached by philosophy can be the same as the God reached through Christian revelation.

IDEAS

Analytical philosophy of religion: tests the adequacy of all theological arguments by the standards of formal logic. The vast assumption of the analytical approach is that theological truth is indeed logical. If theological truth has a rationality which is not simply 'logical' – say, a poetic rationality – then the analytic approach has rather missed the point. Richard Swinburne is the leading exponent of analytical theology.

Apologetics: the defence of theology from its critics.

Philosophical theology: the branch of theology that tries to explain religious belief in rational terms, summed up in St Anselm's motto: 'faith seeking understanding'. Although philosophical theology shares the same subject-matter as the philosophy of religion, philosophical theology aims to defend a theological viewpoint, but the philosophy of religion subjects all theological viewpoints to philosophical questioning and critique.

The Socratic method: the question-and-answer method (or dialectical method) of philosophising used by Socrates. Jesus uses the Socratic method in many of his conversations.

Sophistry: a form of philosophy that tries to advance its case using rhetorical tricks and false reasoning.

Theodicy: the justification of God's ways to humanity.

BOOKS

George Pattison, *A Short Course in the Philosophy or Religion* (SCM, 2001)

Brian Davies (ed.), *Philosophy of Religion: A Guide and Anthology* (OUP, 2000)

Pluralism

Religious pluralism asserts the theological value of more than one religious belief or form of life.

The issue of pluralism goes right back to the discussions of the ancient philosophers about the One and the Many. When we look at the world, it appears as a jumble of many entities, yet we still speak in the singular about 'the world' and our 'experience of the world', as though the vast array of different objects in our field of vision were also united into one thing called 'the world' or 'the cosmos'. The monist assumes that the separate parts of our experience are unified. The pluralist takes the view that the multiplicity of separate things in the world is the true reality: the world is not singular, but composed of many distinct entities.

The phrase 'religious pluralism' is not generally used to mean that there is more than one god (that is 'polytheism'), but that there are *several true understandings* of God. So the pluralist might argue that the Muslim, the Christian and the Jew are all worshipping God in their different ways, as John Hick put it in the book of the same title: 'God has many names.'

Religious pluralism is also not necessarily the same thing as religious relativism. The relativist argues that there are no absolute truths. The pluralist may argue that there is absolute truth, but that it is expressed in many different ways.

The pluralist view may be contrasted with the 'exclusivist' view (which takes one's own religion to be the only true path to God) and the 'inclusivist' view (which allows for the possibility that other religions might be alternative expressions of one's own true religion). So the 'exclusivist' Christian would say that Muslims are wrong; the 'inclusivist' Christian would say that Muslims have found another way of expressing Christian truth; and the 'pluralist' Christian would say that Muslims have an equally valid but different religion.

John Hick offers a 'Kantian' version of pluralism, arguing that God is still one, even if we travel there by different paths. In this way, Hick did not challenge the singular reality of God. Hick's view also made the differences between religions appear insignificant. David Ray Griffin has argued the more radical view that the different religious paths actually lead to different destinations, but that these plural destinations are equally valid. The Muslim path takes you to one place, and the Christian path leads to another. So our separate paths are not just alternative routes to God, but the only means of reaching our particular religious goal.

More radically still, the Catholic theologian Joseph O'Leary (*Religious Pluralism and Christian Truth*, Edinburgh University Press, 1996) has argued that authentic religion must abandon its claim to be absolute: 'Release from ... absolutism requires the insight that neither individuals nor nations nor creeds possess a stable identity unchanging throughout history. What they have instead is a story, a trajectory, in which they are constantly reinventing their identity.'

All pluralist views are anathema to conservative Roman Catholics, who argue that 'outside the Church there is no salvation', and to conservative Evangelicals, who argue that salvation only comes through a relationship with Jesus Christ. Conservatives find it equally difficult to tolerate pluralism within their own religion, insisting on an exclusivist understanding of orthodoxy as rigid dogma from which there can be no deviation.

THINKERS

Wilfred Cantwell-Smith (1916–2000), in *The Meaning and End of Religion* (1963), distinguished between 'faith' and 'belief'. 'Faith' is a trust in God that cuts across religious cultures, whereas 'beliefs' are specific to particular religious communities.

Jacques Dupuis (1923–2005), a Roman Catholic, argued in *Toward a Pluralist Theology of Religions* (1997) that God is also present in other religious traditions. He was cross-examined by the Congregation for the Doctrine of the Faith and was suspended from his position at the Gregorian University.

John Hick (1922–) used Kant's distinction between an object 'in itself' and how it appears in our perception to construct a theory of religious pluralism that distinguishes between God in himself and how he appears to the different world religions: 'Each concrete historical divine personality – Jahweh, the heavenly Father, the Qur'anic Allah – is a joint product of the universal divine presence and a particular historically formed mode of constructive religious imagination' (*Disputed Questions in Theology and the Philosophy of Religion*).

Karl Rahner (1904–84) argued that those of other faiths and none could be included in the Church as 'anonymous Christians'.

IDEAS

Pleroma: the Greek word for 'everything' that is used in the New Testament to mean the fullness of creation.

Trinity: It can be argued that the doctrine of the Trinity (see separate entry) tries to contain both the pluralist and the monist positions in one view of God: God is irreducibly plural yet absolutely singular.

BOOKS

John Hick, *God Has Many Names* (Westminster John Knox Press, 1982)

David Ray Griffin, *Deep Religious Pluralism* (Westminster John Knox Press, 2005)

Post-modern Theology

This term refers to a range of theological responses to 'the post-modern condition' of cultural uncertainty.

The best way to consider 'post-modernism' is in relation to 'modernism'. Modernism (in the sense we are using it here) was characterised by a faith in the human individual and human nature in general; a confidence in science and human reason; and the valuing of historical progress over tradition. Modernism in theology was typified by the nineteenth-century liberal theologians who emphasised the humanity of Jesus and the ethical dimension of Christian life.

It is difficult to date the rise of modernism, but its origins arguably lie in Renaissance humanism, when the authority of the Church was questioned and the individual human being was celebrated as a supreme example of God's creation. The high point of modernism was probably the late nineteenth century, when the progress of human science and technology seemed unstoppable.

Zygmunt Baumann, perhaps the leading commentator on post-modernism, has described modernity as 'an age of artificial order and of grand societal designs, the era of planners, visionaries, and – more generally – "gardeners" who treat society as a virgin plot of land to be expertly designed and then cultivated and doctored to keep the designed form' (*Modernity and the Holocaust*).

The demise of modernism was gradual and took place slowly as a result of a number of catastrophic events in Western history. The destructiveness of the First and Second World Wars undermined both modernism's faith in human nature and its belief in progress. The realisation that our technologies are contributing to risks such as global warming has produced disillusionment with science. And the failure of advanced democracies to tackle long-standing social problems has undermined confidence in our capacity to live up to our own moral ideals.

Post-modernism is not a single reaction but a disorganised collection of responses to the decline of modernism. Modernism undermined our faith in tradition in the name of reason and progress, but the demise of modernism has left us with little confidence in either tradition or human progress.

The post-modern condition, according to Jean-Francois Lyotard, is 'incredulity': we now no longer *believe* either in the old theological certainties or in Enlightenment reason. All the 'big' ideas and 'meta-narratives' have been thrown into question. According to Jürgen Habermas, we live in an age of 'legitimation crisis' when we have no metaphysical or ideological underpinning for our values and aspirations.

As a consequence, we experience what Baumann calls a 'liquid' culture, where our values must be improvised. We no longer have faith in institutions or traditions – religious or otherwise – and connect with others via networks enabled by communications technologies such as the internet.

Post-modern theologies come in many shapes and sizes. There is a growing consensus that, at the very least, post-modernity requires the churches to adopt new strategies and structures. Pete Ward (author of *Liquid Church*), for example, has argued that the Church must learn to connect with networks and emerging cultures rather than remaining holed-up in ecclesiastical structures. More radical thinkers argue that Christianity simply doesn't need formal institutions at all.

Some argue that theology must change radically too, offering people opportunities for encounter, exploration and self-expression rather than dogmatic certainties that are handed down from above.

Some theologians (such as John Caputo) have argued that post-modern incredulity towards God actually makes room for a more true and passionate faith. In a similar vein, Richard Kearney has described God as a 'possibility' rather than an 'actuality'. Carl Raschke has argued in *The Next Reformation: Why Evangelicals Must Embrace Postmodernity* (2004) that the post-modern turn against the secular ideologies of humanism and rationality can provide resources for the renewal of theology.

THINKERS

Don Cupitt (1934–) has argued in a series of books since *Taking Leave of God* (1980) that we need to abandon God in order to recover a theology of 'ordinary language' that finds meaning in everyday experience.

Charles Winquist (1945–2002) proposed a post-modern theology of desire: 'The study of religion is most importantly an experiment in being human' (*The Surface of the Deep*). 'Those for whom I write are restless. They have noted an absence in their lives, but it is not an absence that can be readily filled by institutionalized religion' (*Desiring Theology*).

Zygmunt Baumann (1925–), a leading commentator on postmodernism, sees modernists as 'legislators' who aspired to be architects of a brave new world, and post-modernists as 'interpreters' who attempt to understand the world rather than to change it. He coined the term 'liquid modernity' to describe the uncertain and fluid character of post-modern societies.

Jean-François Lyotard (1924–98): author of *The Post-modern Condition*, which described post-modernity as 'an incredulability towards meta-narratives'.

Edith Wyschogrod (1936–) has argued that the post-modern religious life must now take the form of a quest for saintliness: 'the post-modern saintly life … is a plea for boldness and risk … for a new altruism in an age grown cynical and hardened to catastrophe.'

IDEAS

The Emerging Church: a diverse movement of Christians who believe that in a post-modern culture, religious experience, searching and conversation are more powerful than dogma. As a result, the Emerging Church takes the form of alternative worship, and informal and open-ended organisation.

The Enlightenment project: a term used to describe the modernist faith in historical progress guided by human reason and inventiveness.

Instrumental reason: a term used to describe the aggressive use of reason in the modern period to subjugate nature and society in order to bring about a utopian future.

Late-capitalist: a term used in preference to 'post-modern' by those who see the post-modern era as one in which capitalism has lost its ideological compass.

Late-modern: a term used by some in preference to 'post-modern' because, it is argued, post-modernism is really just an extension of modernist values and practices.

The Liquid Church: an idea, advanced by Pete Ward in a book of the same name, that sees Christianity as a fluid and culturally immersed reality.

Modernism: a term used, in quite different senses, to refer both to a specific artistic movement in the early twentieth century and, more loosely, to the values of the entire modern period from the late Renaissance to the present day.

The network society: the idea that post-modern-culture people relate through networks rather than through institutions.

Post-Enlightenment: a term used in preference to 'post-modern' by those who see the 'post-modern' era as defined by the failure of the Enlightenment project.

Post-structuralism: a movement in literary theory that sees linguistic meaning as fluid and purely conventional.

Secularism: See separate entry.

The death of God: See separate entry.

BOOKS

Kevin Vanhoozer, *The Cambridge Companion to Postmodern Theology* (CUP, 2003)

Stuart Sim (ed.), *Icon Dictionary of Postmodernism* (Icon Books, 1998)

William H. Katerberg and Miroslav Volf (eds.), *The Future of Hope: Christian Tradition amid Modernity and Postmodernity* (Eerdmans, 2004)

Process Theology

Argues that God and creation are in a continual process of becoming.

Process theology originated in the twentieth century as the theological development of the metaphysics of the philosopher Alfred North

Whitehead. At the centre of process theology is the vision of the cosmos as motion rather than a *static system*. According to process theologians, there are no static entities because everything in our world is a movement of continual growth and decay.

Whitehead argued that creation was the result of God's 'yearning after concrete fact' – that's to say, God's longing to turn his ideas into concrete reality. The world that God creates is not a static structure but a dynamic process in which free decisions are made. God himself is caught up in the ongoing process, becoming an effect of his own creative action. In Whitehead's term, God is *bipolar*: both cause and effect, past action and future consequence, potentiality and actuality, time-bound and eternal, transcendent and immanent, idea and event.

The cosmos consists of 'actual' events which are partly determined by their relationship to other actual events and partly free and creative. God's creative action is not simply to set the universe in motion (as the Deists had argued). The act of creation is not an event but a continuous succession of interacting events in which God is the guiding principle. In Whitehead's words: 'It is as true to say that the World is immanent in God, as that God is immanent in the World.'

Although process theology is not necessarily Christian, a number of Christian theologians have argued that the process view of God fits much better with the biblical view of a loving creator who is intimately involved in the history of the cosmos. Furthermore, process theism takes time and history seriously, showing how God can be really concerned with the minutiae of an individual human life. Classical theism, by contrast, regards God as 'monopolar': eternal, static, abstract. The 'bipolar' view of process theology means that God is both eternal and completely tied up with the activity of the universe.

Although process theology had its heyday in the 1960s and 1970s, and although the technicalities of process theology are now very much a niche interest in academic theology, the underlying ideas of process theism have exercised a very considerable influence over Anglophone liberal Protestantism from the 1960s onwards.

The principal objection to process theology is that it appears as though Christian theology has merely been bolted onto a process philosophy. Although thinking of theology in terms of process is illuminating, process philosophy works perfectly well without the

Christian God, even without God altogether. Nietzsche and Kazantzakis, for example, have offered staunchly non-theological versions of process philosophy. Unlike most conventional theism, process theology does not depend upon any special revelation, so the teachings in the Bible are supplementary to, rather than essential to, the philosophical understanding of cosmic process.

It is possible to argue that the logical conclusion of process theology is the kind of post-Christian process theology set out by Don Cupitt, who argues that the world is in a continual flux of becoming, but a flux without God.

THINKERS

Henri Bergson (1859–1941) argued that we experience the world as 'duration', the simultaneous happening of events in time.

John Cobb (1925–): a leading process theologian who tried to 'understand faith in Christ as demanding openness to others' and 'identified Christ with creative transformation' (*Christ in a Pluralistic Age*, 1975).

Don Cupitt (1935–) argues that 'we should see the whole of reality as like a great fountain that continually recycles its own waters … It is composed of nothing but a pure formless rush of contingency, pouring out and scattering' (*The Religion of Being*, 1998).

David Ray Griffin (1939–): a leading process theologian who has argued for a post-modern process theology of nature in which the human subject is understood within the context of an ecological whole. The task of theology should be 'to relate talk of nature, human nature and divine action to contemporary sciences' (David Ray Griffin and Houston Smith, *Primordial Truth and Postmodern Theology*, 1989).

Charles Hartshorne (1897–2000) developed Whitehead's philosophy as a theological system. Hartshorne's God is absolute in the sense of being 'unsurpassable', but this does not stop God surpassing himself. He is the 'self-surpassing surpasser' who develops in time. Hartshorne differs from Whitehead in thinking of God as a 'society of actualities' rather than a single actuality.

Heraclitus (sixth century BC) argued that everything in the cosmos is in continual change, hence his famous dictum: 'You never step in the same river twice.'

Nikos Kazantzakis (1885–1957): a Greek novelist, author of *The Last Temptation of Christ*. Kazantzakis believed that life is a process of heroic struggle: 'My prayer is not the whimpering of a beggar nor a confession of love. Nor is it the petty reckoning of a small tradesman: Give me and I shall give you. My prayer is the report of a soldier to his general: This is what I did today, this is how I fought to save the entire battle in my own sector, these are the obstacles I encountered, this is how I plan to fight tomorrow' (*The Saviors of God: Spiritual Exercises*).

Friedrich Nietzsche (1844–1900) argued that the cosmos is 'a monster of energy, without beginning, without end … at the same time one and many … eternally changing, eternally flooding back … with an ebb and flood of its forms … this, my Dionysian world of the eternally self-creating, the eternally self-destroying' (*The Will to Power*).

Norman Pittenger (1905–97) argued that the God of process theology is closer to the biblical picture of God than the static God of classical theism: 'Every theology must have some final criterion. Paul Tillich has "the new being", biblical fundamentalism had "the word of Scripture"; liberalism, in the older mode, appealed to "experience". Process theology finds its criterion in the biblical text, "God is love".'

Alfred North Whitehead (1861–1947) set out a philosophy and metaphysics of process that formed the basis of later process theology.

IDEAS

Actual entity (or actual occasion): the description of entities as events that we experience in time.

Panentheism (literally 'everything in God'): the belief that God is infused in the cosmos.

BOOKS

David Ray Griffin and John Cobb, *Process Theology: an Introductory Exposition* (Westminster Press, 1976)

C. Robert Mesle, *Process Theology: a Basic Introduction* (Chalice Press, 1993)

Proofs for the Existence of God

Arguments that attempt to demonstrate beyond question that God exists.

One of the main preoccupations of theology has been whether it is possible to prove the existence of God. These proofs have fallen into two broad categories: analytical proofs modelled on mathematics, and empirical proofs that argue that God can be deduced from our experience.

The most famous analytical proof was the 'ontological argument' first devised by St Anselm and subsequently revised by Descartes, Leibniz and, in our own age, Charles Hartshorne and Alvin Plantigna. In a nutshell, the ontological argument states that it is contradictory to think that a perfect being would not exist. This is because a non-existent perfect being would be imperfect, and therefore absurd. Thus a perfect being exists necessarily by virtue of its perfection.

The classic version of the argument runs in three stages, like this: (1) God, by definition, must possess all the perfect attributes. (2) Existence is more perfect than non-existence. (3) Therefore God must possess the attribute of existence. It was this version of the argument that Immanuel Kant demolished so spectacularly in his *Critique of Pure Reason*. He said that 'existence is not a predicate' that can be added to the concept of a thing. In other words, existence is not an 'attribute' that God can possess alongside his omnipotence, omniscience and so on. So when we say 'God is', we are not adding anything real to our understanding of him.

Although Kant's critique left the ontological proof in ruins for two centuries, there was a revival of interest in the argument in the twentieth century. Charles Hartshorne (1897–2000) argued that we only need to *exclude* God's impossibility or meaninglessness in order to establish his reality. God's impossibility can be excluded because the idea of God *must* include his existence. (The idea of a non-existent God, says Hartshorne, is *not an idea of God*.) It is not necessary to think the idea of God, but if we do, we necessarily assume God's reality.

The best-known empirical argument for God is the so-called 'argument from design'. If we look around at the world, with all its complex organisms and physical structures, it exhibits qualities of design: order, regularity and purpose. These features point to the existence of a designer/God.

David Hume attacked the design argument (*The Dialogues Concerning Natural Religion*), saying that we cannot use an analogy from human experience of design and apply it to God. In one of his many witty arguments against the design theory, Hume offers a *reductio ad absurdam*, saying that the world has qualities of vegetative propagation, rather than mechanical design. This would point towards the existence of a vegetable God spawning a vegetable cosmos.

The debate about the design argument runs and runs. Although Darwin's evolutionary theory seemed to put paid to the idea that complex biological structures must have been designed by God, the development of the 'anthropic principle' in cosmology has (in some people's minds, at least) given the design argument new scientific credibility.

The argument from design is enjoying a controversial revival in right-wing Christian circles, where it is argued that the universe exhibits 'intelligent design'. This idea has been rubbished by neo-Darwinists like Richard Dawkins and Daniel Dennett. The debate goes on.

The problem with 'proofs' for God's existence is that they tend to be religiously unsatisfying and reduce the issue of God to a logical puzzle. It may also be argued that proof of God's existence diminishes faith, as Douglas Adams put it in *The Hitchhiker's Guide to the Galaxy*: "'I refuse to prove that I exist,' says God, "for proof denies faith, and without faith I am nothing.'"

THINKERS

Thomas Aquinas (1224–74) offered 'five ways' to prove God's existence, including arguments from design and first cause (see 'The cosmological argument' below).

Søren Kierkegaard (1813–55) argued that the existence of God cannot be proven by reason. Instead, one should have faith in God even if this belief seems to be absurd.

Charles Darwin (1809–82) invented the theory of evolution, which said that the living world had not been created but had evolved from primitive biological forms.

Immanuel Kant (1724–1804) argued that the analytical proofs for God's existence all collapse into the ontological argument, which he 'disproved' (see above). He was less critical of the design argument, but did not think that the establishment of 'a designer' was sufficient to prove the existence of God.

William Paley (1743–1805) devised the watchmaker argument (see below) in his *Natural Theology* (1802).

IDEAS

The anthropic principle states that the physical conditions of the universe are precisely those required for carbon-based life to flourish. This points to the improbability of human life merely being a coincidence.

The cosmological argument, first advanced by Aristotle, said that God must be 'the first cause' of all the events and entities in the universe.

Pascal's wager: Blaise Pascal's argument that belief in God is rational because the risks of not believing in God (possible damnation) outweigh the risks of believing in him.

The teleological argument: another term for the design argument.

The watchmaker argument: a version of the design argument, which reasoned that if you found a watch lying on a beach, you would assume the existence of a watchmaker.

BOOKS

John Barrow and Frank Tipler, *The Anthropic Cosmological Principle* (Oxford University Press, 1986)

Richard Swinburne, *The Existence of God* (Oxford University Press, 1979)

Radical Orthodoxy

The view of orthodoxy as an 'organic language of tradition' which has been marginalised by secular modernity.

The Radical Orthodoxy movement in theology began in the 1990s with a group of Cambridge academics inspired by the theologian John Milbank. His *Theology and Social Theory* (1990) was a landmark text, setting out what he saw as the fatal errors of modern Christian theology, along with his remedy: radical orthodoxy.

In Milbank's analysis, everything started to go wrong with theology in the thirteenth century – in particular, with the theology of Duns Scotus. From this time people started to think of the world as a secular space within which human beings could act as free creators, designing their own societies and planning their futures without reference to God. Before this time (according to Milbank's thesis) there was an assumed theology of 'participation' which saw everything and everybody as part of God's creation. So in pre-modern times, there was no 'secular' world and all human life was regarded as part of God's creative activity.

According to Milbank, the consequences of secularisation have been devastating, turning human beings from creatures 'made in God's image' into isolated individuals who act out their lives on a secular stage, imposing their will upon nature and other human beings. The divine pre-modern world, participating in the life of God, was replaced by a disenchanted human existence. Milbank describes secularism as 'nihilistic' because it is disconnected from the real divine source of meaning and value. Instead of challenging this nihilistic secularism, liberal theologians have, says Milbank, colluded with it, effectively de-Christianising Christianity.

For Milbank, post-modernism provides Western Christendom with a unique opportunity, because we are at last acknowledging the failure of modern secular ideologies. In this context it is possible to assert once more the pre-modern Christian world-view of divine participation. Milbank argues that Christianity must rediscover its orthodox identity by returning to the shared mythic narrative of

Christianity: its rituals, stories and practices. This orthodoxy is 'radical' because it challenges and subverts the received wisdom and values of secular culture.

One of the effects of secular thinking has been the dethroning of theology from its ancient status as 'Queen of the Sciences'. Theology now has to jostle in an unseemly way with all kinds of secular disciplines. Milbank argues that theology is not just another way of thinking, on a par with the natural or social sciences. If theological claims are truly theological – if theology is really talking about the divine foundation of all reality – then theological thinking must logically precede every other kind of discourse.

Since the mid 1990s Radical Orthodoxy has become increasingly popular among young theologians. But it has also been subject to criticism. Milbank's sweeping historical analysis of the rise of secularism has raised a few eyebrows. Others have argued that Radical Orthodoxy is really just an activity for a select band of academics and that (unlike, say, the nineteenth-century Oxford Movement) it has failed to inspire any notable examples of Christian practice.

The long-term impact of Radical Orthodoxy remains to be seen. No one can doubt the stimulus that it has provided to contemporary theology. But it is doubtful whether there is sufficient vitality in the ideas to make any difference to the fate of Western Christendom.

THINKERS

John Milbank (1952–): the leading thinker in Radical Orthodoxy.

Catherine Pickstock (1970–): one of the founding theologians of Radical Orthodoxy. She has argued for the importance of liturgy in understanding the concept of 'participation'.

Graham Ward (1955–): one of the founding theologians of Radical Orthodoxy.

IDEAS

Mythos: a term used by Milbank to designate the narrative nature of the Christian tradition.

Non-identical repetition: the idea that orthodoxy must perpetuate itself by repeating its historic rituals, stories and practices, but always in a new time and in new cultural circumstances.

Participation: a term used to describe the way that everything we experience in life participates in the life of God.

Secular reason (or 'instrumental reason'): the use of reason for purely human ends.

BOOKS

John Milbank, Catherine Pickstock and Graham Ward (eds.), *Radical Orthodoxy, A New Theology* (Routledge, 1999)

Douglas Hedley and Wayne Hankey (eds.), *Deconstructing Radical Orthodoxy* (Ashgate, 2005)

Religious Language

The status of religious language or 'God talk' has been an issue since the beginning of Christian theology.

The question of the status of religious language, or how we speak about God, has, implicitly or explicitly, been at the centre of all Christian theology. This is because religious language is the basic medium for formal theology.

The problem of religious language is raised in the first place by the texts of Scripture: how do they speak about God? Origen, one of the first academic theologians, argued that Scripture is essentially allegorical rather than literal, speaking about God in figures and metaphors. He shared the Platonic view that language is a poor substitute for pure thought, and saw allegory as a way of moving beyond words into a hidden realm of pure spiritual meaning.

The Platonist view that language cannot express God or truth finds its most powerful religious form in the Christian mystics, particularly the negative theologians, who believed that we have to let go of language in order to contemplate God.

In the Middle Ages, the question of religious language was raised again by Thomas Aquinas, who wanted to explain how language could talk positively about God. Aquinas argued that we cannot speak in a precise (univocal) way about God because our languages are imperfect. However, our talk of God is not entirely false (equivocal) either. Religious language has the status of analogy, so when we speak of God as Father, we do not think that he is literally our father, but we do accept that he is our father in an analogous sense. This is true for all our religious language: our statements about divine love, truth, justice and so on, are analogies of God's real love, truth and justice. In this way Aquinas established a powerful general theory of the way in which religious language works.

In the twentieth century a number of conflicting theories have been advanced. Karl Barth argued strongly against the theory of analogy, saying that words cannot speak about God except by grace, which operates miraculously to make our theological languages meaningful. Religious language only works because God chooses to reveal himself in it.

The logical positivists, notably A. J. Ayer, argued that the word 'God' is meaningless because statements about God can never be verified, or indeed falsified. The phrase 'God is good' is an article of faith which cannot be 'checked out', therefore having as much real meaning as the phrase 'X is good'. Ian Ramsey (in *Religious Language*) responded to the positivists by arguing that talk about God is in fact anchored in the 'religious situation' of the speaker.

In the latter half of the twentieth century, the so-called post-structuralist theory of language opened up a new understanding of God-talk. The post-structuralists (and others like Ludwig Wittgenstein) argued that language is a fluid system in which the meaning of words is never stable. We have no choice but to understand our world, and God, within free-floating networks of linguistic meaning. This controversial theory argues that God-talk takes its meaning not from reference to God, but from the underlying system of human language.

Although few theologians have adopted a full-blown post-structuralist theory of language, the influence of post-structuralism has been immense and most theologians now accept that languages operate flexibly within cultures.

THINKERS

Don Cupitt (1934–) argues (in *The Long Legged Fly*) that religious language says nothing about God, who doesn't exist, but functions to provide us with a sense of cosmic order, purpose and values.

Jacques Derrida (1930–2004) argued that all languages are systems of differential signs (or *différance*) in which there are no absolute meanings. Derrida suggested (very tentatively) that God might be the reality of language itself rather than just a concept within language.

Ludwig Wittgenstein (1889–1951) developed the theory of language games (see below). He once said that the essence of religion does not lie in the meaning of language, but in the act of using language: 'Thus it does not matter if the words used are true or false or nonsense.'

IDEAS

Allegory: a story in which the characters, events, objects and locations refer to other realities. The parable of the prodigal son, for example, is an allegory of God's forgiveness.

The doctrine of analogy: the theory (developed by Aquinas) that human words operate as analogies to divine realities.

Glossolalia: the Christian practice of 'speaking in tongues' which was common in the early Church and is now widespread among Charismatic and Pentecostal churches.

Language games: the theory (invented by Ludwig Wittgenstein in the early twentieth century) that particular instances of language can only be understood within the context of language games, and that these games always have a cultural setting or 'form of life'.

Metaphor: a figure of speech in which the meaning of a word is 'carried over' and used in a different context. 'God is a rock' is a metaphor.

Pentecost: an event described in the book of Acts, when the apostles spoke to a crowd of people from different countries, but their speech was understood by all.

Speech act theory: the idea (advanced in the 1960s by John Searle and John Austin) that language communicates through the way it is 'performed'.

Symbolism: a word or image that stands for some other thing. For example, the sun is often used as a symbol of Christ.

The Tower of Babel: a mythical tower (described in the Old Testament) which was built to give humans access to God. God demolished the tower and punished humanity by making it speak in different languages.

BOOKS

Ian Ramsey, *Religious Language* (SCM, 1957)
Dan Stiver, *The Philosophy of Religious Language: Sign, Symbol and Story* (Blackwells, 1996)

Revelation

Revelation is the disclosure of God, his message and his purposes.

The English word 'revelation' is derived from the Latin *revelare*, meaning 'to remove a veil'. In the New Testament the Greek word for revelation is *apocalypsis*, which also means 'unveiling'.

In the Old Testament God reveals himself through miraculous events (such as the burning bush) and through the words of the prophets. In the New Testament, Jesus himself is the most perfect revelation of God, but God also discloses himself in other ways: in visions to Paul and the Apostles, through the agency of angels, and through the work of the Holy Spirit in the life of the early Church.

In post-biblical times Christians have believed that God reveals himself supremely in the Scriptures. This does not rule out the possibility that God can reveal himself in the life of the Church, through the use of human reason, and through the events of human history. But Scripture, as the direct word of God, is generally used as the test of the veracity of other forms of revelation.

Theologians distinguish between different kinds of revelation theology. The term 'revealed theology' is used to describe the revelation of God's word in Scripture. Scripture is taken to contain the revelation of the truths necessary for salvation. Martin Luther emphasised the primacy of revealed theology in Scripture, as did Karl Barth.

The term 'natural theology' (see separate entry) is used to describe the revelation of God in the processes of the world, including the exercise of human reason. This means that God can reveal himself to anyone, not only to Christian readers of the Bible. Thus Augustine believed that God had revealed himself in the philosophy of Plato, and Aquinas believed that God had revealed himself through the philosophy of Aristotle.

From the early nineteenth century, with the rise of historical consciousness (an awareness that we all exist in history), theologians started to think more about God's revelation through the events of human history. For example, Hegel argued that the whole of human history was the working out of the mind or spirit of God. Hegelian ideas were strongly resisted by Karl Barth (and his successors), whose 'dialectical' theology argued that God's word enters human history, rather than being an internal part of history.

THINKERS

Emil Brunner (1889–1966) argued that revelation is not just a list of doctrines handed down from heaven, but a 'personal correspondence' or 'encounter' between God and humanity: 'God does not reveal this and that – he reveals himself by communicating himself.'

The Cambridge Platonists (seventeenth century): a group of theologians, based in Cambridge, who argued that God reveals himself inwardly to the human mind and soul: 'The spirit in man is the candle of the Lord.'

Avery Dulles (1918–): an orthodox Roman Catholic theologian who set out, in his *Models of Revelation*, five types of Christian revelation: Doctrine (the teaching of the Church as God's communication of truth); History (the events of history as the disclosure of God's purposes); Inner Experience (mystical or other inward encounters with God); Dialectical Presence (God revealed in the relationship between the reader and Scripture); and New Awareness (where God is revealed in the raised consciousness of the believer).

H. Richard Niebuhr (1894–1962) argued in *The Meaning of Revelation* (1941) that God reveals himself in a dimension between the inner spiritual experience of God (internal history) and the outward events of world affairs (external history): 'External history is the medium in which internal history exists and comes to life.' Thus the absolute revelation of God appears within the contingent and relative processes of human history.

IDEAS

Epiphany: a Greek word meaning a 'showing', which is used to describe a special moment of revelation.

General revelation: rather like 'natural theology', this is a term used to describe the universal revelation of God in the world. This revelation is accessible to everyone, of every religion and none, simply by being human and experiencing the wonder and beauty of the cosmos. Liberal theologians (see separate entry) tend to emphasise the importance of general revelation as a way of including all faiths, indeed all humanity, in the understanding of God.

The hiddenness of God: the idea that God can only reveal himself by not revealing himself. We find the concept powerfully expressed in the Old Testament: as the book of Isaiah says, 'truly you are a God who hides himself' (Isa. 45:25). According to the doctrine of hiddenness, God must always remain hidden from our understanding even as he reveals himself, because we could not possibly comprehend the reality of God.

Kenosis: the idea that God 'emptied himself' in order to become human in Jesus Christ.

Offenbarsein: the concept of 'revealedness' used by Karl Barth to describe the process by which God's self-revelation becomes apparent to us through the mediation of the Holy Spirit.

Special revelation refers to the particular revelation of God through culturally and historically specific people and occasions: for example, Scriptures, religious teachers and historical events. Conservative theologians argue that God has made a special revelation to Christians and that this revelation is the ultimate and saving truth. (See 'General revelation' above.)

BOOKS

Avery Dulles, *Models of Revelation* (Orbis Books, 1992)

Gerhard Sauter and John Barton (eds.), *Revelation and Story* (Ashgate, 2000)

Paul Avis (ed.), *Divine Revelation* (Eerdmans, 1997)

Sacrament

A visible sign of God's grace.

The word 'sacrament' comes from the Latin *sacramentum*, meaning 'a pledge of faithfulness' made by a Roman soldier. But in Christian theology, 'sacrament' refers to God's self-disclosure through specific signs and ceremonies.

In the widest sense a sacrament is any event which provides us with a sense of God's presence or grace. In this general sense, anything or any experience could be sacramental. Indeed, one might speak in a universal way about a sacramental dimension in all of creation. Albert Blackwell has argued in *The Sacred in Music* that music is sacramental. Urs von Balthasar has argued that poetry can function as a sacrament and cites Gerard Manley Hopkins as an example.

In the narrower sense the sacraments are officially sanctioned rites which are administered by ordained ministers of the Church. In this sense the sacraments belong exclusively within the life of Church. In the Orthodox and Catholic churches there are seven official sacraments: baptism, confirmation, marriage, eucharist, holy orders, anointing the sick and penance. Protestant churches recognise only two: baptism and eucharist. The official (or ordained) sacraments are administered by the ordained clergy.

Although the question of how the sacraments work is generally declared to be a 'mystery', efforts have nevertheless been made to explain it. The classic explanation was offered by Thomas Aquinas, who used Aristotle's distinction between 'substance' and 'accident' to explain that the eucharistic elements of body and blood are Christ's 'substance' appearing under the material guise ('accidents') of bread and wine.

Jesus himself is described as the primordial sacrament, from whom the other sacraments derive their divine efficacy. So the

121

sacraments are not human symbols to express our ideas about God. They are, rather, actual instances of God's grace. The sacraments do not function only as signposts to a God who is somewhere else; they are taken to be the locations of God's presence. As the Catholic catechism puts it, sacraments are 'masterworks of God'. They are acts of God, not signs of God.

It is also misleading to think of the sacraments merely as 'windows' onto some other world. St Augustine makes this mistake when he says that 'the spiritual virtue of a sacrament is like light; although it passes among the impure, it is not polluted.' Augustine's Platonic view gives no value to the living material of the sacrament, only to some meaning that passes through it. A more satisfactory theology of the sacraments sees the sacrament itself as a living instance of God's grace.

THINKERS

St Thomas Aquinas (1225–74) argued that only the seven 'ordained sacraments' are truly sacramental, although he allowed that many things may be non-sacramental 'signs of God'.

Jean-Pierre de Caussade (1675–1751) wrote a book popularly known as *The Sacrament of the Present Moment* (originally *The Self-abandonment to Divine Providence*) in which he argued that time itself is sacramental, and that the ordinary Christian has direct access to sacramental experience without the mediation of a priesthood.

Peter Lombard (c. 1100–1160) wrote about the sacraments in his work *The Sentences*. Using Aristotelian theory of causation, Lombard argued that four 'causes' must be operating for a sacrament to exist: there must be a 'material cause' (e.g. the bread and wine for the Eucharist); a 'formal cause' (the liturgical words that accompany the administration of the sacrament); the 'efficient cause' (the presence of a priest); and a 'final cause' (the communication of God's grace to the recipient of the sacrament).

Henri de Lubac (1896–1991) argued that the sacraments validate the Church rather than vice versa. The Church becomes itself properly through the Eucharist.

Karl Rahner (1904–84) described the Church as the 'primal sacrament' on which the others are grounded.

IDEAS

Mysterion ('hidden reality'): a word for 'sacrament' used by the Eastern churches.

Sacramentary: a book containing the prayers that the priest recited at the celebration of the Eucharist.

BOOKS

John MacQuarrie, *A Guide to the Sacraments* (Continuum, 1997)
Edward Schillebeeckx, *Christ the Sacrament of the Encounter with God* (Sheed & Ward, 1963)

Scriptural Reasoning

A form of discussion between the Abrahamic faiths, rooted in the practice of discussing Scripture together.

Scriptural Reasoning (hereafter SR) is a form of inter-faith discussion based on the shared reading of Scripture. SR builds upon the foundation of Scripture and traditions that the Abrahamic faiths (Judaism, Christianity and Islam) have in common. Fundamental to SR is the presupposition that reasoning can only take place adequately in the light of scriptural revelation.

Although SR appears to be a neo-conservative practice appealing to the special revelation in Scripture, there are many features of SR which are quite radical, or have radical implications. It is implicit in SR that those of some other faiths have an equally valid claim to religious truth and that, at some stage in the future, some kind of reconciliation of the faiths will be possible. SR also implicitly rejects dogmatic ideas of truth in favour of truths which emerge in specific human contexts, within historically located human conversations, and within interpretive communities. So truth is dynamic, rather than static, and unfolds in many forms as Scripture is read and re-read.

The idea of a form of reason that operates in communal discussion plugs into a wider contemporary debate about the nature of reason. Jürgen Habermas, the German philosopher, has argued against the post-modern assumption that there are no norms of reason and that one idea of reason is as good as any other. Habermas argues that there is what he calls a 'systems rationality': a form of reason that arises from human conversation about the truth. For Habermas, reason is not the activity of a solitary mind (as the Enlightenment tradition from Descartes had presumed) but takes place in community as people talk with each other about what is valuable, true and real.

SR owes something to Habermas' social theory of reason, because it sees reason disclosing itself in dialogue. But whereas Habermas sees reason as a purely human activity, SR believes that reason has been revealed by God both in Scripture and in traditions of human science and thinking. In asserting that the discussion of scriptural revelation can be a form of reason, SR sets itself against the secular model of reason as an individual mental activity that requires no religious revelation.

Indeed SR is a self-conscious response to what it sees as the restrictive and dogmatic understanding of reason bequeathed to us by the Enlightenment. SR poses the possibility that there are many different forms of logic and that the narrow logic of scientific reasoning is not deep or broad enough to deal with the complex reality of human existence. This is not such a strange idea: we speak about 'reasons of the heart' and 'poetic reasoning' as legitimate forms of human reasoning. The difference with SR is the priority that it gives to specific scriptures in the understanding of reasoning.

SR also sets itself at a distance from the liberal understanding of reason as a universal human activity. By making reason the subject of a special scriptural revelation, SR restricts the full disclosure of reason to those inside the closed circle of scriptural reasoners.

THINKERS

Jürgen Habermas (1929–) argues that the norm of reason is a form of conversation that he calls the 'ideal speech situation', an imaginary state of affairs in which all the parties to a conversation would have equal, unrestricted opportunity of participation. Habermas has provided an important counter-voice to the often fashionable 'post-modern' consensus that it is no longer possible to disentangle truth from fiction.

Peter Ochs (1950–): a Jewish theologian who is the leading figure in Scriptural Reasoning: 'The purpose of SR is to recover the practice of listening for the speech of God that both preceded and still provides the terms for modern thinking.'

IDEAS

Hypothesis formation: the idea (from C. S. Peirce, the American pragmatist philosopher) that the exploration of likely hypotheses is a form of logical reasoning. SR sees its task as not so much to disprove what it sees as the flawed rationality of the secular world, as to hypothecate theological alternatives to secular modernity.

BOOKS

David Ford and C. C. Pecknold (eds.), *The Promise of Scriptural Reasoning* (Blackwell, 2006)

Nicholas Adams, *Habermas and Theology* (Cambridge University Press, 2006)

Peter Ochs, 'Returning to Scripture: Trends in Postcritical Interpretation', *Crosscurrents*, Winter 1994/95, Vol. 44, Issue 4

Secularisation

The replacement of religious world-views with non-religious patterns of life and thought.

The word 'secular' comes from the Latin *saeculum*, meaning 'the present age', and is often contrasted with the concept of 'the sacred'. Sacred things come from God, whereas secular things are the products of human activity.

This distinction, as we will see, is open to the objection that human activity is also God-given and that the 'secular world' doesn't really exist: everything is already God's world. This view has been argued persuasively by John Milbank and the Radical Orthodoxy school of theology.

The concept of 'secularisation' came to prominence with Max Weber, who tried to analyse the decline of religion in the West. He wrote about 'the disenchantment of the world' as people increasingly rejected a religious understanding of life in favour of 'rational' scientific, economic, psychological and sociological explanations. Secularisation is now applied in a less technical sense to describe all encroachments on religion: from the separation of Church and State in the USA to the introduction of Sunday trading in the UK.

Broadly speaking, secularisation theorists have divided along two lines. There are those like Karl Löwith, who argued that secularisation is the non-religious development of Christian salvation history. On this view, the Christian commitment to the kingdom of God is transformed into a secular desire to build a perfect society on earth. So secularisation is taken, in essence, to be a Christian development.

In the other camp are those like Hans Blumenberg (*The Legitimacy of the Modern Age*, 1966), who has argued that the Enlightenment marks a decisive break with earlier Christian ideas. For Blumenberg, secular culture has its origins in the steady development of scientific and cultural 'curiosity': 'there arises in the modern age an indissoluble connecting link between our historical self-understanding … and our claim to unrestricted theoretical curiosity.'

Critics of 'secularisation theory' (as it has come to be called) throw up a host of objections. It is said that secularism doesn't exist as a coherent ideology because it is simply the rejection – in numerous contradictory forms – of religious life. So the Marxist and the atheist capitalist can both be called 'secularists'. Others have pointed out that the truth of secularisation theory depends upon an unproven historical assumption that religious feeling really has declined in the West. Furthermore, secularisation theory offers no explanation for the current rise in neo-conservative and fundamentalist religions.

Liberal theologians tend to welcome many aspects of secularism. They agree with the secular contempt for superstition and admire the secular concern with human rights. They applaud the use of science to save and improve life. But liberal theology is not in vogue. The current neo-conservative trend is to regard all secular initiatives with suspicion and to insist that all truth must come through the Church.

THINKERS

Karl Barth (1886–1968) saw the process of modernity as a process of secularisation in which humanistic values displaced the centrality of God.

Peter L. Berger (1929–) argued in *A Rumor of Angels* (1969) that believers are now a 'cognitive minority' struggling against a growing secular consensus.

Hans Blumenberg (1920–96) argued in *The Legitimacy of the Modern Age* (against Löwith and others) that secularism is not an extension of salvation history, but the liberating development of a non-Christian humanism.

Dietrich Bonhoeffer (1906–45) recommended a religionless, worldly Christianity.

Harvey Cox (1929–) argued in *The Secular City* that we must stop using the word 'God' in order to rediscover the real God in the political struggles of the world.

Wilhelm Dilthey (1831–11) argued that secularisation is the result of our awareness of 'human nature' and the evolution of 'natural', non-religious forms of society and government. Human life is a secular quest for individual 'meaning'.

George Holyoake (1817–1906): founder of the Secular Society, who first used the term 'secularism' as the name of his philosophical system. (See also 'Atheism'.)

Immanuel Kant (1724–1804) coined the term 'enlightenment' to describe 'man's emergence from his self-incurred immaturity … The motto of enlightenment is therefore: *Sapere aude*! Have courage to use your *own* understanding.'

Karl Löwith (1897–1973) argued that the modern period was motivated by a Christian impulse to realise heaven on earth.

Karl Marx (1818–83) argued that religion would naturally wither as people's real needs were met by the communist state.

Wolfhart Pannenberg (1928–) has argued that many secular developments (such as the creation of 'human rights' and an increasing concern with individual human welfare) complement Christian teaching.

Max Weber (1864–1920) traced the origins of secularisation to the Calvinist work ethic which formed the basis of Western capitalism.

IDEAS

The National Secular Society: a campaigning organisation that is opposed to religion in general.

Secular Christianity: a number of theologians in the 1960s (for example, Paul van Buren, Harvey Cox and Gregor Smith) argued that Christianity must become more secular, abandoning traditional religious language and seeking to express Christian values through human values and structures. Secular Christianity is seen by some as a golden age of radical theology and by others as the final suicidal act of liberal Protestantism.

BOOKS

David Martin, *A General Theory of Secularization* (Harper & Row, 1979)

Sin

Sin is an act or state of disobedience against God.

The New Testament Greek verb *harmartano*, translated as 'to sin', literally means 'to miss' a target – and by extension, 'to fall short' of a moral standard.

In its simplest sense, 'sin' is the transgression of divine law: the breach of rules. Thus murder, theft and adultery are all sins because they are forbidden in the ten commandments. In a broader sense, sins are any deviation from God's will. Jesus teaches, for example, that even *thinking* about a breach of divine law is a sinful action, even if no law is broken. So sin is also any ungodly state of mind or motivation or attitude.

More than this, though, Christianity has regarded sin as a state of being: we do not merely commit sinful acts and harbour sinful thoughts, we are sinful in our very being. Even when we are striving with every intention of being good, we cannot overcome our basic state of sinfulness. This idea is called 'the doctrine of original sin'.

In its naïve, literal form the doctrine of original sin states that the act of disobedience of Adam and Eve in the Garden of Eden was an historical event: there really was an apple, a snake and a tree of knowledge. Because of Adam and Eve's crime, the whole of humanity was placed in a state of sin. So, according to the doctrine, every person is born with a moral defect. Original sin is not an action that we can apologise for, but an ingrained feature of human nature. We can only be saved from original sin by God's grace.

The doctrine is open to numerous objections. Since the mid nineteenth century, the historical truth of the Genesis story has been completely discredited and is now only believed by cranks and fundamentalists. Much earlier, in the fifth century, Pelagius argued that there was no 'original sin' and that sinfulness in the human world had come about through bad moral habits. He believed that the doctrine of original sin, which says we can do nothing to help ourselves, would encourage moral complacency.

The doctrine is also regarded as barbaric by many modern people. The idea that God holds every person in history responsible for the sins of two people paints God as an absurd and unjust tyrant. Similarly, the idea that newly-born infants are 'sinful' is, on the face of it, deeply objectionable. Original sin has been seen by some liberation theologians as an instrument of priestly power over the faithful. Others have said that the doctrine of original sin reflects dysfunctional Christian attitudes to sexuality and the body, leading to a destructive psychology of self-loathing.

More radically, some thinkers have argued that the so-called 'original sin' was not a sin at all, but a moment of human liberation. Erich Fromm argued, for example, that 'the act of disobedience set Adam and Eve free and opened their eyes ... "Original sin," far from corrupting man, set him free; it was the beginning of history. Man had to leave the Garden of Eden in order to learn to rely on his own powers and to become fully human' (*The Heart of Man: Its Genius For Good and Evil*, 1964). A similar view has been expressed by Philip Pullman in the *His Dark Materials* trilogy.

The foremost modern advocate of the doctrine of original sin was Reinhold Niebuhr, who argued that the doctrine needs to be understood as a factual description of the human condition: 'Original sin is that thing about man which makes him capable of conceiving of his own perfection and incapable of achieving it.' So original sin is not something we need to feel personally guilty about. However, we should acknowledge the truth of our human moral incapacity.

Niebuhr criticised modern culture for preaching a naïve doctrine of human goodness which completely ignored the 'mystery of evil in human life': 'The utopian illusions and sentimental aberrations of modern liberal culture are really all derived from the basic error of negating the fact of original sin.' Niebuhr's theology has been severely criticised by neo-orthodox Barthians, such as Stanley Hauerwas, for trying to make Christian doctrine acceptable to modern liberal culture.

Whatever view we take, it is hard to see how Christianity can be credible without an adequate theory of tragedy. If we accept that the world is full of moral failure and that our own lives are imperfect (as we surely must), then we require a theory of tragedy in order to make sense of human existence. Secular thinkers like Marx and Freud, having dispensed with Christian ideas of sin, were forced to reinvent the concept in the form of a theory of alienation (Marx) and the death drive (Freud).

THINKERS

St Augustine (354–430) is credited, unfairly, with 'inventing' the doctrine of original sin. He was, however, the classic exponent of the doctrine.

Tissa Balasuriya (1924–): a Sri Lankan theologian, who was excommunicated by the Roman Catholic Church in 1997 for allegedly denying the doctrine of original sin (along with other doctrinal 'errors' in *Mary and Human Liberation*, Mowbray, 1997). Balasuriya argued that he had 'no difficulty with original sin in the sense of a human proneness to evil', but objected to the use of the doctrine as an instrument of oppression.

Matthew Fox (1940–) argued in *Original Blessing* (1983) that the doctrine of original sin has been given too much prominence and that God's original blessing of the earth is what really defines human existence.

Ernest Gellner (1925–95) offered a psychological interpretation, arguing that we never start life with a clean slate, because we contain within us complex unconscious material: 'the unconscious is a new version of original sin' (*The Psychoanalytic Movement*, 1985).

St Paul (3–65) set out ideas of original sin in the letter to the Romans: 'sin came into the world through one man' (Rom. 5:12). Paul emphasised death as the consequence of Adam's sin.

Jonathan Swift (1667–1745) in *Gulliver's Travels* showed the corruption of humanity in the depiction of the 'Yahoos', a race obsessed by excrement, sex and cruelty.

IDEAS

Cheap grace: a term coined by Dietrich Bonhoeffer to describe the view of grace that expects no reciprocal sacrifice from us: 'Cheap grace means the justification of sin without the justification of the sinner. Grace alone does everything, they say, and so everything can remain as it was before.'

Efficacious grace: the idea that God's grace overpowers our will.

False guilt: guilt for something we are not responsible for.

Felix culpa: the idea that the original sin of Adam and Even was a 'happy fault' because, without this transgression, Jesus would not have been required as a Saviour.

Grace is God's freely given generosity towards humanity which is believed to release humanity from sin.

Jansenism argued that there is no grace outside the Church.

Mortal sin: according to Roman Catholic teaching, this is a deliberate, knowing and serious act of sin that results in eternal damnation.

The seven deadly sins: pride, avarice, lust, envy, gluttony, wrath, sloth.

Sufficient grace: the idea that God gives us sufficient assistance to overcome sin, but that our own free decision is still required.

Venial sin: according to Roman Catholic teaching, this is a sin that can still be redeemed by God's grace following a period of punishment in purgatory.

BOOKS

James Alison, *The Joy of Being Wrong: Original Sin Through Easter Eyes* (Crossroad, 1998)

Reinhold Niebuhr, *Moral Man and Immoral Society* (Continuum, 2005)

Marjorie Suchocki, *The Fall to Violence: Original Sin in Relational Theology* (Continuum, 1995)

Tatha Wiley, *Original Sin: Origins, Developments, Contemporary Meanings* (Paulist Press, 2002)

The Soul

An inner spiritual dimension within each human being.

Concepts of an inner spirit, soul, self or consciousness have been crucial to the Christian understanding of what it means to be human. And although most theologians would confidently say that we do possess an inner spiritual identity, fewer would be able to explain satisfactorily exactly what this inner person is, and how it relates to our physical bodies.

In Jewish and early Christian thought, the soul was not regarded as a distinctively spiritual substance. Genesis refers to God blowing the breath of life (*ruah*) into the physical body to create a living human being, and this concept of 'breath' continues into the New Testament, where the 'spirit' is called *pneuma* – a life force acting like wind or breath. But *pneuma* is physical stuff and not fundamentally different from the physical substance of the body.

The dualistic view of humans as body and spirit has its roots in the thinking of Plato, who regarded the soul as immortal and the body as a temporary physical container for use during the earthly phase of our existence. The Platonic soul is composed of three parts: reason (*nous*); noble desire (*thymos*) and appetite (*epithemia*). In the Phaedrus, Plato compares the soul to a chariot with two horses. The first horse is focused and full of noble desire, the second is skittish and is pulled this way and that by its appetites. The charioteer represents reason (*nous*), which must ensure that the horses pull in the same direction, towards a worthy goal such as truth, or justice, or love.

Aristotle took Plato's basic concept, but tried to show how the soul relates to the body, arguing that the soul is the 'form' or 'idea' of the body. Like Plato, Aristotle believed that the soul was best governed by reason.

The dominant Platonic–Christian dualistic view was given new vigour in the seventeenth century by Descartes, who argued that the world is made up of two kinds of substance: 'thought' and 'extension' (i.e. 'physical form'). Descartes was unable to demonstrate how the soul and its thoughts are connected with the body, and subsequent philosophers tried to address this problem. In particular, the Jewish theologian Baruch Spinoza developed Aristotle's thinking in order to overcome Descartes' dualism. Spinoza argued that the soul and the body are flip-sides (different 'modes') of the human person, and not separate substances. The soul is the person considered from the point of view of 'thought', and the body is the same person considered from the point of view of 'extension'.

Some scientists and philosophers of consciousness argue that there is no reason to posit the existence of an inner human spirit or self. David Hume argued that the self is just the sum of its sensual perceptions, and a similar view is held today by the American philosopher Daniel Dennett, who sees no special 'problem' with consciousness: consciousness is simply the brain's response to stimuli. Even a thermometer has a conscious 'self', says Dennett, because it is aware of different thermal states. Evolutionary biology (and not God) explains how our complex human consciousness has developed.

Dennett's emphasis on biology is significant, even if we do not reach his atheistic conclusions. Western Christianity has vastly over-emphasised the spiritual dimension of the relationship with the divine: the individual soul connecting with God's spiritual reality. The physical world is too often regarded as the mere clothing for our spiritual existence, a regrettable necessity rather than something with equal religious significance. After all, we human beings do not merely *have* bodies, we *are* bodies.

As a corrective, modern theologians are now paying attention to theologies of the body. Pope John Paul II, for example, published *The Theology of the Body*, affirming the integrated view of the human person as mind, soul and body. Although a welcome move towards the

Christian affirmation of physical human existence, John Paul's theology was still dominated by conservative ideas about sexuality. More radically, some theologians (see James Nelson below) have affirmed the physical body as the primary means by which we relate to God and each other.

That we are embodied creatures can hardly be denied, but we do also have the experience of an inner identity and personhood which is not manifest in our bodies. We all experience an inner life – of thoughts, feelings and perceptions – which is crucial to what we mean by our 'self'. We believe that this inner person can exercise freedom and make choices about how our bodies will behave. We also believe that the identity of this inner person remains continuous even as our bodies change radically from birth to old age. Although the theology of the body is an important development, the puzzle of the human soul, self or spirit will surely persist as one of the basic questions of human existence.

THINKERS

Pierre Teilhard de Chardin (1881–1995) emphasised the materiality of creation: 'The prevailing view has been that the body ... is a *fragment* of the Universe, a piece completely detached from the rest and handed over to a spirit that informs it. In the future we shall have to say that the Body is the very Universality of things ... *My matter* is not a part of the Universe that I possess totaliter: it is the *totality* of the Universe possessed by me *partialiter*' (*Science and Christ*, Harper & Row, 1968).

James B. Nelson (1930–) has argued that bodily experience must be the starting point for theology: 'Christian faith at its core is about the embodiment of God in our own daily flesh-and-blood encounters' (*Between Two Gardens*, Pilgrim Press, 1983).

Gilbert Ryle (1900–1976) argued in *The Concept of Mind* (1949) that consciousness can be explained without having to posit the existence of a 'ghost in the machine'.

IDEAS

Anima: the Latin word for 'soul'.

Bundle theory: from David Hume, the idea that the self is not an entity but 'a bundle or collection of different perceptions'.

Mind–body identity: the idea that the mind is a physical part of the body.

Mind–body problem: the difficulty of explaining how an immaterial world of thought can connect with the material world of physical objects.

Monad: a concept most closely associated with Leibniz, who argued that the world is made up of basic spiritual entities (monads).

Pre-existence of souls: the Platonic concept (supported by the Christian theologian Origen) that the soul exists before being incarnated into a body.

Problem of other minds: the difficulty of knowing whether other people really have minds like ours, when we can only observe their bodies.

Psyche: the Greek word for the 'spirit' or the spark of life.

Traducianism: the idea that one's soul, like one's body, is derived through natural generation from one's parents.

Transcendental ego: a term used by Kant and others to describe the inner self which synthesises all our conscious experiences.

BOOKS

James B. Nelson, *Body Theology* (Westminster/John Knox, 1992)

Anthony Kenny, *The Anatomy of the Soul: Historical Essays in the Philosophy of Mind* (Blackwell, 1973)

Lisa Isherwood and Elizabeth Stuart (eds.), *Introducing Body Theology* (Pilgrim Press, 2000)

Systematic Theology

The attempt to produce a total theological system covering everything from creation to the end of the world.

There are many ways to express theological truth: in music, through poetry and painting, through rituals and stories. Systematic theology tries to express religious truth in an exhaustive system that covers every aspect of theology. Founded on the belief that God is unified and coherent, systematic theologies have attempted to produce a unified and coherent account of everything to do with God and his creation.

Unfortunately, the Bible was not written in a systematic way and does not speak with one voice. With some exceptions, such as Paul's letters, the Bible presents stories rather than structured arguments. So any systematic theology must to some extent coerce the biblical material into a formal structure. This creates a basic and unavoidable tension between 'systematic' and 'biblical' theology. For some, such as Walter Brueggeman, this is a fatal flaw in all systematic theology.

Although the beginnings of systematic theology can be seen as early as Origen's *De Principiis* (arguably the first comprehensive system of Christian dogma), systematic theology came into its own in the Scholastic period, most famously in St Thomas Aquinas' (uncompleted) *Summa Theologica*, which used Aristotle's philosophy of Being to produce a total theory of God and existence. In the late nineteenth and early twentieth centuries, there was a German revival in systematic theology, with monumental projects from a range of theologians including Ritschl, Barth, Tillich and Rahner.

Most systematic theologies rest upon a central insight or argument. Aquinas argued that theology must be understood in terms of concrete existence rather than abstract ideas. For Calvin, the absolute sovereignty of God is the central concept. In Barth, the revelation of God's word is the governing principle. For Tillich, theology must begin with the question of human existence. But if the governing principles of a systematic theology are discredited or rejected, the whole system is instantly called into question.

Although there are theologians who are still writing systematic theology (for example, James William McClendon), the post-modern suspicion of 'ideology' means that all grand systems of thought have lost their attraction. Barth's *Church Dogmatics* was a magnificent achievement and its influence has been immense. But like the last great battleships, it was, in retrospect, a project that belonged to the past rather than the future.

Systematic theological thought in general has ceased to be valued for various reasons. The very word 'system' now has sinister over-tones, suggesting an oppressive restriction of individual theological freedom. Many of the more political theologians see the task of theology as precisely to subvert all human 'systems' on the grounds that they lead to totalitarianism. Furthermore, ordinary faith doesn't present itself in a systematic way, but takes the form of a story with many unpredictable twists and turns. Many people find more religious value in mystical or practical theologies that offer nuggets of wisdom and parables, than in volumes of theological analysis. They might easily say, with some justification, that Jesus was a wisdom teacher of precisely this kind.

For the time being systematic theology has been eclipsed by various narrative theologies, both conservative and liberal, that see the coherence of Christianity in its guiding stories rather than in an overarching theory.

THINKERS

Karl Barth (1886–1968) wrote his *Church Dogmatics* in reaction to the failure of liberal theology in the face of Hitler's Nazism. The project was never completed but still runs to 12 volumes, each averaging more than 600 pages. It is interesting that even Barth warned that 'systematization is always the enemy of true theology.'

John Calvin (1509–64) wrote the *Institutes of the Christian Religion*, which was the first Protestant systematic theology.

Marsilio Ficino (1433–99) wrote a *Platonic Theology* which consisted of 18 volumes.

John of Damascus (700–760) wrote *The Fountain of Wisdom* in an attempt to bring together in one compendium all the accrued wisdom of the Church Fathers.

Peter Lombard (1100–1160) was the first great systematiser of the Western Church, and his *Sentences* tried to collect together in a single work the wisdom of the Church Fathers.

John Milbank (1952–) has argued that Christianity is structured by the repetition and performance of a narrative that he calls 'the Christian mythos'.

Paul Tillich (1886–1965) produced a systematic theology based on the insights of existentialism.

David Tracy (1939–) has emphasised the importance of 'the fragment' – or unsystematic truths – in contemporary theology and culture.

IDEAS

Biblical theology is usually contrasted with systematic theology and refers to the unsystematic theology of the Bible.

Dogmatic theology or dogmatics: the attempt to justify orthodox Christian belief.

Mystical theology is generally *unsystematic*: poetic, aphoristic and narrative.

Unsystematic theologians: many theologians have not felt it necessary to produce formal systems – Martin Luther, for example.

BOOKS

Wolfhart Pannenberg, *Introduction to Systematic Theology* (Eerdmans, 1991)

Theism

> The theory that a God (or gods) exist(s). Theism is not necessarily a religious belief, although it may form part of religious belief.

The word 'theism' is derived from *theos*, the Greek word for 'god'. Theism is the theory that a God, or gods, exist(s). As a theory, it is reached by the exercise of human thought. So theism is, strictly speaking, just an intellectual position, not an act of religious belief. By contrast, religious faith in God depends upon God revealing himself in ways that may not be rational or comprehensible – 'faith believes nor questions how'. (See 'Negative Theology'.)

Theism is one of those apparently simple words that conceal a great muddle of ideas and beliefs. When we use the word 'theism' we need to be clear what we are saying. Ideas of God are immensely varied and it makes little sense to lump them all under the heading of 'theism', as though all forms of belief in God were somehow the same. This would put Christianity, Satanism and Hinduism all in the same category.

To avoid confusion, the word 'theism' really needs to be reserved for a philosophical or intellectual belief in God based upon arguments and reasoning. (Otherwise all our vocabulary becomes too imprecise to be useful.) The tradition of considering God in this way goes back to the ancient Greek philosophers, particularly Plato and Aristotle. Plato argued that God (or 'the Good', as he called it) was the most perfect of all perfect ideas. Aristotle also thought God was supremely rational, but introduced the idea that God was the 'unmoved mover' instigating the process of all the events of cosmic history. Plato had an immense influence on Christian ideas of God, particularly through St Augustine, who described Platonism as 'Christianity for the masses'. Aristotle's critical influence on Christian thought came 1000 years later, when St Thomas Aquinas developed his controversial theology of Being, which drew heavily upon Aristotle (whom Aquinas referred to simply as The Philosopher). Aristotle's ideas also surface in the seventeenth-century Jewish theology of Spinoza.

The question of whether belief in a God can be justified rationally has been an issue for theology since the earliest times. Justyn Martyr, for example, in the early second century, saw God as the Logos, or the fount of reason. In recent times Richard Swinburne is probably the best-known proponent of rational theism. He argues that theism is both logical and coherent, because God offers the best way of making sense of the whole of our experience. On the other side, there have been plenty of philosophers – notably A. J. Ayer, Anthony Flew and Richard Hare – who have argued that belief in God can never be verified and is therefore irrational and meaningless. Interestingly, in 2004 Anthony Flew changed his mind and said that he did believe in God after all: 'I'm thinking of a God ... in the sense of a being that has intelligence and a purpose.'

Theistic belief does not necessarily translate into religious conviction. The desire to worship God does not necessarily follow from the fact that we give intellectual assent to the idea of a perfect being.

THINKERS

Ralph Cudworth (1617–88): one of the so-called Cambridge Platonists. He probably coined the term 'theism'.

Jacques Derrida (1930–2004) argued that 'we should stop thinking about God as someone, over there, way up there, transcendent, and, what is more … capable, more than any satellite orbiting in space, of seeing into the most secret of the most interior of places' (*The Gift of Death*). Instead, we should see God as 'the structure of conscience'.

Georg W. F. Hegel (1770–1831) believed that God was a 'mind' or 'spirit' guiding history towards a rational future.

David Hume (1711–76) argued in *The Dialogues Concerning Natural Religion* that belief in God is not rational.

Immanuel Kant (1724–1804) held the theistic view that God is a necessary (or 'regulative') 'idea', but could find no value in arguments for God's existence.

John Locke (1632–1704) argued in *The Reasonableness of Christianity* that the religious truths revealed in Scripture could also be verified by using human reason.

Isaac Newton (1642–1727) believed that the mind of God could be glimpsed through the logical scientific laws of the universe.

Alvin Plantinga (1932–) argues that theism is 'warranted' because it is 'a properly basic belief'. If God created us in such a way that we should believe in him, then belief in God would be rational, even if there were no evidence for it and our arguments were not very good.

Baruch Spinoza (1632–77) held the monist view that God (or Nature) is the one substance out of which the universe is made.

Richard Swinburne (1934–) argues that belief in the Christian God provides the best possible explanation for our experience of the world.

IDEAS

Agnosticism: the belief that it is not possible to say whether God is real or not.

Atheism: the belief that there is no God of any kind. Socrates (470–399 BC) was arguably the first thinker to be accused of 'atheism'. (See 'Atheism'.)

Deism: the belief (dominant in the Enlightenment) that the reality of God as the 'author of nature' or 'supreme being' can be demonstrated by reason. The Deist God sets up the laws of the universe but does not interfere with human affairs.

Dystheism: the belief that God exists but is malevolent.

Eutheism: the belief that God exists and is good.

God of the gaps: the use of God to fill the gaps in the scientific explanation of the cosmos.

God of the philosophers: a phrase used to describe a purely intellectual belief in God without any living religious faith.

Monotheism: the belief that there is only one God.

Nihilism: the atheistic belief that there are no ultimate meanings. (See 'The Death of God'.)

Ontological argument: a rational argument for God's existence which was first suggested by St Anselm. (See 'Proofs for the Existence of God'.)

Open theism: the view, developed by Clark H. Pinnock (1940–) and others, that God is open and responsive to his creation.

Panentheism (literally 'everything in God'): the belief that God is infused in the cosmos.

Pantheism: the belief that God is the same thing as the universe.

Polytheism: the belief that there is more than one god.

BOOKS

M. Diamond and T. Litzenburg (eds.), *The Logic of God: Theology and Verification* (Macmillan, 1975)

Paul Copan and Paul K. Moser (eds.), *The Rationality of Theism* (Routledge, 2003)

Theological Ethics

Ethics worked out from theological principles or revealed truths.

Religious people of all kinds have believed that they are in receipt of special insights about how to live an ethical life. God is seen to impart laws, wisdom, ethical principles, conscience or God's own Spirit to enable us to behave righteously.

A central dilemma in all ethics is how to reconcile the need 'to do the right thing' (deontological ethics – see below) with the need 'to bring about the right consequences' (consequentialist ethics – see below). On the one hand, we would say, as a matter of principle, that it is not right to hurt another human being. On the other hand, the surgeon who refused ever to hurt his patients would cause more harm than good. So on one side we have the application of principles, the need to fulfil duties, the requirements of law, and the importance of proper motivation. And on the other side we have the need to bring about good outcomes.

In the modern period Christian ethics has come under three main influences. The first is the consequentialist ethics of the Enlightenment, which had as its goal the creation of a better (or even a perfect) world-order. Christian socialists, philanthropists, and social reformers argued that the task of ethics was to be *effective* in building the New Jerusalem on earth. Good intentions were all very well, but they believed that the churches had a leading role to play in the improvement of society.

The second influence is the individualism of modern and post-modern culture. This has produced an increasingly subjective and personalised ethical vision, based upon the satisfaction of individual needs, preferences and judgements. We now think of society in terms of individuals pursuing their ends, rather than communities working out the rules and ethos of their common life.

Thirdly, the modern period has been increasingly dominated by ethical reasoning based on individual 'rights'. The traditional Christian ethic of responsibility for one's neighbour has been largely replaced in public ethical discussion by the question of how we fulfil our neighbour's rights. So the ethic of the Good Samaritan who was 'moved' to act by the plight of his neighbour has evolved into a functional ethic that requires no real compassion for others, so long as our neighbour's entitlements to food, shelter and medical care are met.

There have been a range of reactions to these cultural shifts. Liberal theologians have tended to see what is implicitly Christian in the ethics of secular modernity, and have affirmed that. Karl Barth argued that all ethics must be the application of divinely revealed principles, values and laws. Alasdair MacIntyre, for example, has argued that we need to return to a distinctively Christian ethic of virtue. We cannot base our ethics upon calculations of the probable consequences of our actions. Rather, we should strive after the virtues that St Paul lists in the New Testament: 'The fruit of the Spirit is love, joy, peace, patience, kindness, goodness, faithfulness, gentleness and self-control' (Gal. 5:22–23).

More radical voices have urged us to move beyond theological ethics altogether. Bishop Richard Holloway has advocated 'godless morality': 'it is better to leave God out of the moral debate' and find 'good human reasons' for supporting our ethical viewpoints. Holloway argues that ethics is like musical improvisation – we take the traditional Christian ethical tunes and make new music out of them.

THINKERS

Aristotle (384–322 BC) was concerned with how to live a good life (*eudaimonia*, the way of living leading to excellence). The good life depends partly upon natural virtue (one's innate character), partly on moral virtue (one's habits of behaviour), and partly on reason (which regulates and moderates our emotions). Aristotle's ethics are 'teleological' (see below) because they are directed towards the practical goal of excellence.

Immanuel Kant (1724–1804) argued for a deontological ethic of duty. For Kant, only universal ethical principles were rational, and this formed his famous 'Categorical Imperative': 'Act only according to that maxim by which you can at the same time will that it should become a universal law.'

Alasdair MacIntyre (1929–): a Catholic moral philosopher who argues that we have lost an adequate vocabulary for discussing ethical issues. He urges us to return to the virtues – or 'practices' – for our ethical vocabulary and to a communitarian approach that allows the discussion of shared values.

Simone Weil (1909–43): a French philosopher who was exceptionally scrupulous in her ethical approach, arguing that we must not cause any harm to others. Weil starved herself to death in solidarity with French soldiers suffering in World War II.

IDEAS

Antinomianism: the belief that the right course of action will be supplied by the Holy Spirit, or some other form of inspiration.

Casuistry: the adaptation of ethical principles to suit specific circumstances.

Consequentialist ethics (or teleological ethics or utilitarian ethics): an ethical approach based upon the outcomes, goals or consequences of an action. Actions are 'good' if they bring about a good outcome. Consequentialism allows that 'the end justifies the means'. So, by contrast with the deontologist, the consequentialist argues that it may be right to do the wrong thing in order to bring about a good outcome.

Deontological ethics: the view, expressed by Kant, that we act ethically when we fulfil our Christian duty to love, forgive, act justly, and so on. Kant argued that right actions are right universally and not merely in particular circumstances. This means that it is always correct to 'do the right thing' even if the situation appears to demand otherwise.

Dialogical ethics: a procedural approach to ethics, advocated by Jürgen Habermas, which takes right and wrong to be the product of cultural conversation. Right and wrong are thus decided at any given time by the prevailing consensus. The task of the dialogical ethicist is to set the rules of dialogue, rather than to insist on a particular outcome.

Imitation of Christ: the ancient ethic, set out by Thomas à Kempis (fifteenth century), of emulating Christ in one's approach to life. The contemporary practice of asking 'What would Jesus do?' (WWJD?) is a modern version of the imitation of Christ.

Moral realism/ethical realism: the belief that our values are given objectively.

Moral scepticism: the view – expressed, for example, by John Mackie in *Ethics: Inventing Right and Wrong* – that 'there are no objective values'.

Quandary ethics: a form of moral reasoning which gives priority to the consideration of complex and apparently insoluble dilemmas.

Situation ethics: the application of ethical principles in specific contexts. The best-known Christian situationist is Joseph Fletcher (1905–91): 'The situationist enters into every decision-making situation fully armed with the ethical maxims of his community and its heritage, and he treats them with respect as illuminator of his problems. Just the same he is prepared in any situation to compromise them or set them aside *in the situation* if love seems better served by doing so' (*Situation Ethics*, 1966).

The Good: in Plato's philosophy, the ultimate ethical reality.

Theocratic ethics (or divine command ethics): the view that we can only do the right thing by following direct commands from God set out in Scripture or elsewhere.

Virtue ethics (or character ethics): the view that the goal of ethics is to cultivate the Christian virtues within ourselves and apply these virtues appropriately in our daily living. Alasdair MacIntyre and Stanley Hauerwas advocated this view.

Virtues: admirable human characteristics that distinguish good people from bad.

Voluntarism: in ethics, the belief that right conduct derives from the expression of God's will.

BOOKS

Gilbert Meilaender and William Werpehowski, *The Oxford Handbook of Theological Ethics* (OUP, 2005)

James H. Burtness, *Consequences: Morality, Ethics, and the Future* (Fortress Press, 1999)

Richard Holloway, *Godless Morality* (Canongate, 1999)

Anders Nygren, *Agape and Eros* (University of Chicago Press, 1982)

Alasdair MacIntyre, *After Virtue* (Notre Dame Press, 1984)

Theological Realism

The belief that God exists independently of our ideas about him.

On the face of it, the assertion that 'God is real' would seem to be basic to any Christian theology. However, the question of God's reality is not straightforward. On the one hand, God necessarily surpasses our conceptions of reality; on the other hand, God's reality must somehow connect with ours if we are to have any knowledge of him. So how we speak of divine reality is a theological puzzle.

Christian theology has, very broadly speaking, been an uneasy combination of the Jewish conception of God as the force guiding human history, and the Platonic conception of God as eternal and unchanging truth. Thus God is spoken of as being supremely real for us both in the flesh-and-blood historical figure of Jesus Christ, and as a 'transcendent', 'immortal' and 'invisible' deity. When we speak of God's transcendent reality, we appear to deny his immanent reality, and vice versa.

Thomas Aquinas tried to reconcile the tension between the transcendent and immanent dimensions of God's reality by arguing that God's reality (Being) underpins our reality (being): 'To be everywhere primarily and per se belongs to God, and is proper to Him, because whatever number of places be supposed to exist, God must be in all of them, not as to part of him, but as to his very self.' In this way our reality is intimately connected with God's.

The philosophy of Immanuel Kant (1724–1804) marked a watershed in Western thinking about the reality of God. Before Kant, theologians had worked on the assumption that God really existed 'out there' as a supernatural being. Because God was assumed to exist, it was reasonable enough for theologians to attempt to describe God's attributes and speculate about where and how in the cosmos God might exist.

Kant is significant because he undermined the old supernatural idea of God and replaced it with the idea that God is only real within human life and consciousness. Kant argued that it is beyond the power of reason to demonstrate the supernatural reality of God (see 'Proofs for the Existence of God'). The best we can say of God, argued Kant, is that he is an *idea* that we can't do without. We need the idea of God if we are to make sense of the rest of our experience. Thus with Kant, the question of the reality of God merged with the question of how we make sense of our existence both theoretically and practically. In other words, theology became a special way of reflecting upon the human condition.

The emergence of Kantian philosophy coincided with stunning discoveries in the natural sciences that were threatening to make God redundant to the explanation of the physical universe. If science can explain the processes of the natural world, then (Kant had implied) God may only be needed to help us understand how to behave in the world (ethics) and how to give meaning to our lives (aesthetics).

In the centuries that followed Kant, the question of God's existence was replaced more and more by the question of human language about God. Instead of asking, 'Is God real?' theologians asked, 'In what sense does the *word* "God" refer to something real?' This subtle but crucial shift opened up the possibility that the word 'God' is merely expressive of something real, without having to say that God himself is real.

Thus 'God' was said to express our 'highest ideals', or our 'ultimate concern' (as Paul Tillich put it), or 'the ground of our being' (John Robinson), or just 'life' itself. In this way, many theologians stopped trying to prove or describe (or even believe in) the reality of God. Instead they used the word 'God' as a way of categorising dimensions of human experience. God lost his own independent reality status, and became part of our human reality.

Despite a vociferous conservative backlash from theologians like Karl Barth, the Kantian theological paradigm still dominated the twentieth century. The ultimate summary of Kant's theology was made by Don Cupitt in his landmark book *Taking Leave of God* (1980). Cupitt argued that God 'is the religious demand and ideal, the pearl of great price and the enshriner of values. He is needed – but as a myth.' Cupitt has since moved beyond this position to argue that God is not really needed at all, and that non-theistic ideas of 'being' and 'life' may provide us with a better vocabulary for making sense of things.

It could be argued that calling God 'real' involves a category mistake. God doesn't need to be 'real', he just needs to be God, because being God is much better than merely being 'real'. Indeed, as many philosophers have pointed out, God is not so much 'real' as the guarantee of what is real. Saying 'God is real' is like saying 'God exists': it doesn't tell us anything about him. The question then is not whether God is 'real' but whether we trust that God is God. It all comes down to faith.

THINKERS

George Berkeley (1685–1753) was the arch-idealist, arguing that God causes our *experiences* of the world to be real, but that the world itself is not real. So as you read this text, it appears to be real. But all that is real is the idea you have of reality.

Don Cupitt (1935–) has argued for a position called 'non-realism'. This means that the world is only as real as it appears to be, and there is no metaphysical reality hidden behind the manifest world.

Michael Dummett (1925–): an anti-realist philosopher who has argued that a statement can only true or false when we have agreed in advance the means by which the truth of the statement can be verified. So there is no such thing as 'reality' out there that our words refer to. Instead, calling something 'real' is an agreed way of speaking about things: 'We are entitled to say that a statement P must either be true or false ... only when P is a statement of such a kind that we could in a finite time bring ourselves into a position in which we were justified in either asserting or denying P; that is when P is an effectively decidable statement' ('Truth' in Michael Dummett, *Truth and Other Enigmas*).

G. E. Moore (1873–1958) described himself as a 'natural realist', defending the 'common sense' view that the external world is objectively real.

D. Z. Phillips (1934–2006): a Wittgensteinian philosopher of religion who argued that since God is not 'real', language about God cannot explain anything. However, religious language does function as part of a 'form of life' which is real and does have meaning.

Hilary Putnam (1926–): in *Reason, Truth and History* (1981) he abandoned his early metaphysical realism in favour of what he called 'internal realism', meaning that reality is constituted in our internal structures of cognition. There is no 'God's eye view' of reality, said Putnam, only our human perspectives. This leaves open the possibility of more than one 'true' version of reality.

Richard Swinburne (1934–) argues that it is rational to believe that God is real because belief in God's reality makes best sense of the full range of human experience.

IDEAS

Constructivism: the belief that we construct reality (collectively and individually) within culture and language.

Critical realism: the belief that some aspects of our experience are real and others are not. The critical realist maintains that God is real at the same time as arguing that the languages used to speak about God are cultural constructs.

Empiricism: the belief that all knowledge derives from information received via the senses.

Fideism: the belief that the reality of God can only be grasped by faith.

Idealism: the belief that reality is constituted in human consciousness. (See 'George Berkeley' above.)

Metaphysical realism: the belief that the reality of the world is objective and independent of the way that we view and interpret the world.

Narrative realism: the belief that God's reality takes the form of the story of his relationship with the world.

Nominalism: the belief that so-called 'universal concepts' have no reality. For example, 'green' is a universal concept embracing all green objects. We may say that green objects exist, but the nominalist says that 'green' per se does not exist. So individual things are real, but the categories (universals) to which they belong are not real.

Non-realism: the belief that our ideas of reality are human inventions.

Positivism: the belief, dominant in the natural sciences, that the physical world is real and provides us with the basis of all knowledge.

Religious realism: the belief that God is real for those who believe in him.

Speech Act Theory: the theory that words are also actions, and the meaning of words depends upon the act of speech in which they are used. For example, the phrase, 'Let there be light!' means more than the sum of its individual word-meanings; it must also be understood as the speech act of giving a command.

Textualism: another term for constructivism.

BOOKS

Andrew Moore, *Realism and Christian Faith: God, Grammar, and Meaning* (CUP, 2003)

Peter Byrne, *God and Realism* (Ashgate, 2003)

Tradition

The inherited beliefs and practices of the Church.

In theology, the word 'tradition' is used specifically to refer to the inherited beliefs and practices of the Church. The idea of a tradition, which must be treasured and handed down, originates in the New Testament. St Paul refers to what he 'received from the Lord' and delivered to the churches.

According to the conservative interpretation of the word 'tradition', it refers to the body of doctrine that has allegedly been handed down from Jesus via the apostles to the present day. According to the liberal interpretation, there is not one tradition but many, and traditions must be interpreted every bit as carefully as sacred texts.

More radical theological voices have actively challenged the traditions of the Church, subjecting all inherited teaching and practice to a so-called 'hermeneutic of suspicion' which actively suspects the tradition of being oppressive to women and other excluded groups. 'Tradition' is regarded as a tool of ecclesiastical control and power.

The idea that the traditions of the Church can be an authoritative guide to present Christian life depends upon the view that the Church itself is the vehicle for God's revelation. So the traditions of the Church are regarded not simply as the accumulation of its habits and attitudes, but as the expression of the will of God. Thus, conservatives argue that the lack of precedent for women bishops is an argument against them.

The difficulty with this rigid view of tradition is that nothing can change, thus locking God up in the cage of the existing habits of the Church and denying him the opportunity to do anything new. By contrast with the static view of traditions, liberals and modernisers argue that tradition is organic, and that through the dynamic processes of tradition God can bring about new beliefs and practices.

The Roman Catholic and Orthodox churches have laid much greater stress upon the importance of tradition than the Protestant churches, who regard Scripture itself as the overriding authority in all things.

The Anglican Church has affirmed the importance of reason, Scripture and tradition as the three principal sources of religious truth: Scripture is read in the light of tradition and reason; reason in the light of Scripture and tradition; and tradition in the light of reason and Scripture.

The Anglican approach is attributed to the seventeenth-century theologian Richard Hooker, who argued that 'what Scripture doth plainly deliver, to that first place both of credit and obedience is due; the next whereunto is whatsoever any man can necessarily conclude by force of reason; after these the voice of the Church succeedeth. That which the Church by her ecclesiastical authority shall probably think and define to be true or good, must in congruity of reason over-rule all other inferior judgments whatsoever' (*Laws of Ecclesiastical Polity*).

THINKERS

John Milbank (1952–) has argued that there needs to be a recovery of the pre-modern traditions of Christianity. The way to find an authentic Christianity, argues Milbank, is to enact the traditions.

IDEAS

Apostolic succession: the belief, precious to the Roman Catholic Church, that all authentic bishops are direct successors of the first apostles and can trace their lineage right back to Jesus himself.

Paradosis: the New Testament Greek word for 'tradition', meaning 'what is transmitted'.

The magisterium (or the Congregation for the Doctrine of the Faith) has the task of defining and protecting the traditional doctrines and practices of the Roman Catholic Church.

Detraditionalisation: the contemporary 'individualistic' attitude that regards no corporate traditions as sacred, but subjects all traditions to critique, or simply ignores them.

BOOKS

Yves Congar, *The Meaning of Tradition* (Ignatius Press, 2004)

Nicholas Lash, Paul Heelas and Paul Morris (eds.), *Detraditionalisation: Identity in an Age of Cultural Anxiety* (Blackwell, 1997)

Transcendence

Our sense of a divine reality beyond the apparent world.

'Transcendence' means literally 'what is beyond', and in theology it refers to a dimension of divine reality that exceeds everything we can sense or know. To speak of God as 'transcendent' is to say that he is outside of and beyond the world – as it is expressed in the hymn:

> Immortal, invisible, God only wise,
> In light inaccessible hid from our eyes.

The transcendence of God is complemented in most theologies by the idea of God's immanence, meaning God's presence within the world. Most orthodox theology argues that God is both transcendent and immanent. If we suggest that he is purely transcendent, we end up with an utterly remote and unknowable God. If, on the other hand, we suggest that God is purely immanent, we reduce God to something this-worldly.

In the Old Testament the transcendence of God is described in physical terms. For example, God says to Job (Job 38): 'can you bind the chains of the Pleiades or loose the cords of Orion?' The Old Testament God is materially transcendent, a creator whose physical power, majesty and glory exceed anything we can do or know. He stands physically aloof, speaking through the burning bush or the whirlwind. Even Moses is not permitted to see God's face but only glimpses his 'hindquarters' (Exod. 33).

In the New Testament God's transcendence is more spiritual and intellectual: 'no one comprehends the thoughts of God except the Spirit of God' (1 Cor. 2:11). St Paul sees Christ as the bridge to God's transcendence, because Christians have 'the mind of Christ' and have been drawn into God's mysteries and purposes.

Plato's classical idea of transcendence provided the perfect philosophical basis for a Christian theology of God's transcendence. For Plato, the highest level of reality is called the 'The Good', which is 'beyond being' (*epekeina tes ousias* – *The Republic*, 508b) and therefore beyond human cognition and description. A number of neo-Platonic theologians – for example, Proclus and Pseudo-Dionysius – conceived God's transcendence as 'beyond being'.

Thomas Aquinas argued that God's transcendence is a necessary consequence of his perfection, which places God beyond us in every possible way. However, there is a remote analogy between our existence and the existence of God, which means that we can speak meaningfully of God's transcendence.

Mystics of various kinds have believed that it is possible to experience God's transcendence through special forms of spirituality and prayer. St Paul said that he had been transported in prayer to the 'third heaven' (2 Cor. 12). The Renaissance Platonists – Ficino, for example – believed that God's transcendence was accessible through rational contemplation.

With Kant, in the eighteenth century, the idea of transcendence took on a whole new realm of meaning. Kant could see no point in trying to investigate transcendent objects beyond human understanding, because we can never know anything about them. The point of philosophy, he said, should be to help us understand the things that we can know, and how knowledge itself is possible. So he reapplied the idea of transcendence, coining the term 'transcendental' to describe the inner structures of thought and meaning that we use to make sense of our experience of the objective world. (To complicate things, Kant continued to use the word 'transcendent' – as opposed to 'transcendental' – to refer to that aspect of the objective world about which we can know nothing.)

Kant's choice of the term 'transcendental' was deliberately provocative, implying that theology was now a question of trying to understand human cognition rather than trying to understand God. So he spoke about a form of this-worldly 'spiritual' experience of wonder, beauty and the immensity of the cosmos that he called 'the sublime'.

Kant's philosophy played a significant part in the modern loss of belief in any idea of divine transcendence and the growing sense, particularly among liberal theologians, that God is completely immanent in the world and its history. This view does not necessarily mean that transcendence is impossible, because transcendence can be thought of – as it is by Gerard Manley Hopkins – as the inner structure of the immanent world. Transcendence is the sheer excess of God's presence in the created order.

Some post-modern theologians have been asking what the word 'transcendence' can now mean in a secular culture. Emmanuel Levinas has suggested that God's transcendence is glimpsed through the otherness of other human beings. Kevin Hart has suggested that Kant's idea of the 'sublime' is in fact a way of speaking about God's transcendence. Graham Ward has suggested that silence may constitute a dimension of divine transcendence.

THINKERS

Karl Barth (1886–1968) reacted against the liberal emphasis on God's immanence, arguing that God is 'Wholly Other': 'The power of God can be detected neither in the world of nature nor in the souls of men. It must not be confounded with any high, exalted, force, known or knowable' (*The Epistle to the Romans*).

Paul Tillich (1886–1965) argued in *The Courage to Be* that God is so utterly transcendent that he is 'the God above God', leaving us in a state of 'absolute faith'. So the Christian must pass through a moment of atheism and meaninglessness to grasp a pure faith beyond 'the God of theism'.

IDEAS

Deism: the view that God is completely transcendent.

Pantheism: the view that God is in everything and therefore not at all transcendent.

Transcendental: an adjective referring to transcendence, but since Kant this word has taken on a technical use referring to structures of knowledge.

Transcendental concepts: Scholastic theologians identified six transcendental concepts: essence (*ens*), unity (*unum*), goodness (*bonum*), truth (*verum*), thing (*res*), and substance (*aliquid*).

Transcendent fall: the Platonic belief that our embodied earthly existence is a 'fall' from a higher disembodied realm of pure form.

BOOKS

Regina Schwartz (ed.), *Transcendence: Philosophy, Literature and Theology Approach the Beyond* (Routledge, 2004)

The Trinity

The unique Christian view that God consists of three 'persons': Father, Son and Holy Spirit.

The Christian doctrine of a three-fold God is one of the most complex theological ideas in any religion. The doctrine says that God is both unified and composed of three distinct 'persons': God the Father (the creator); God the Son, (Jesus Christ); and God the Holy Spirit. As the Athanasian Creed asserts: 'We worship one God in Trinity, and Trinity in Unity ... For there is one person of the Father, another of the Son, and another of the Holy Spirit. But the Godhead of the Father, of the Son, and of the Holy Spirit is all one.'

The word 'Trinity' does not appear in the Bible, which contains no clear statement of trinitarian teaching. However, there are numerous scriptural passages from which the doctrine can be constructed, principally Jesus' instruction to his disciples to baptise 'in the name of the Father, the Son and the Holy Spirit' (Matt. 28:19). The lack of any more direct statement of the Trinity in the Bible has led some – such as Unitarians, Seventh Day Adventists and Christian Scientists – to argue that the doctrine of the Trinity is not biblical, but an invention of the churches. The first known reference to the Trinity is in the writing of Theophilus of Antioch in the late second century AD, who mentions 'the Trinity of God, His Word and His Wisdom'.

The concept of a trinitarian God appears to be logically impossible, and the Church has traditionally described it as a 'mystery' that cannot be penetrated by mere human logic. Again, as the Athanasian Creed puts it: 'The Father incomprehensible, the Son incomprehensible, and the Holy Spirit incomprehensible.'

However, theologians have nevertheless attempted to make sense of the Trinity as best they can. Tertullian was the first to offer an explanation based on the idea that God is unified in substance: 'One substance, three Persons' – a slogan that has served well down the centuries. 'Ontological' theories have argued that the three persons of the Trinity are the same in their very being or essence. 'Economic' theories have argued that the persons of the Trinity must be understood in terms of their role in human history.

Although the problems of trinitarian theology appear to be uniquely Christian, the fundamental issues can be found in pre-Christian Greek philosophy, where the question of reconciling 'the One and the Many' perplexed the pre-Socratic philosophers and their successors. Parmenides argued the 'monist' position that everything in the world is made up of one substance. Heraclitus argued the 'pluralist' view that the universe is composed of many irreconcilable parts.

Christian approaches to the Trinity can also be viewed as tending either to the monist or the pluralist view. Karl Barth, for example, advocated the 'monist' view, emphasising the unity of the Trinity at the expense of the distinctiveness of the separate persons. By contrast, many contemporary theologians are now seeing the pluralist potential of the Trinity as a resource for understanding God's relationship to our plural and diverse culture.

It is significant that the doctrine of the Trinity is claimed by both liberals and conservatives as crucial to their theology. Those in favour of an 'inclusive theology' towards people of differing sexual orientations and those of other faiths, argue that the Trinity shows that God's essence is 'relational' and always concerned to include the other.

THINKERS

Emil Brunner (1889–1966) argued that the earliest Church had no understanding of the Trinity: 'There is no trace of the idea of "three divine persons in one" in the New Testament ... No Apostle would have dreamt of thinking that there are three divine persons ... The mystery of the Trinity proclaimed by the Church did not spring from biblical doctrine' (*Christian Doctrine of God*).

Colin Gunton (1941–2003) argued in *The One, the Three and the Many* (CUP, 1993) that 'a God who contains within himself a form of plurality in relation and creates a world which reflects the richness of his being, can surely enable us better to conceive something of the unity in variety of human culture.'

Catherine LaCugna (1952–97) has argued that the doctrine of the Trinity is not an exercise in abstract metaphysics but a question of our practical relationship with God.

Jürgen Moltmann (1926–) has argued in *The Trinity and the Kingdom: The Doctrine of God* (Augsburg Fortress Press, 1993) that the Trinity provides the ethical model of radical equality and social mutuality for the kingdom of God.

Karl Rahner (1904–84) argued that 'the economic Trinity is the immanent Trinity, and vice versa'. In other words, God's relationship with the world is part of his essential nature.

Maurice Wiles (1923–2005) argued that the doctrine of the Trinity is not biblical and not necessary to Christianity.

John Zizioulas (1931–) argued that God's very being is tied up with communion.

IDEAS

Analogies of the Trinity: numerous analogies of the Trinity have been offered over the centuries. For example: the three sides of a triangle; three intersecting rings; and the three states of water – ice, steam and liquid. (See also 'Psychological and social analogies'.)

The Athanasian Creed: a fourth-century credal statement, principally of the doctrines of the Trinity and the incarnation. Despite its name, the authorship of the creed is not known and is only ascribed to St Athanasius by tradition.

The 'economic Trinity': the roles that the persons of the Trinity play in relation to human history – for example: creator, redeemer, comforter.

The 'hierarchical Trinity': the view, associated with Tertullian, that the Trinity is a hierarchy, with the Father before the Son, and the Son before the Spirit.

Homoousios: a Greek word (meaning 'of the same essence') used in trinitarian theology to indicate that the persons of the Trinity are all essentially made of the same 'stuff'. The Latin-based term for this idea is 'consubstantial'.

Hypostases: from a Greek term meaning a distinct, self-supporting entity. The Trinity is sometimes described as having three hypostases.

The 'immanent Trinity': God's eternal Trinitarian being in himself. (See also 'The ontological Trinity'.)

The Latin model of the Trinity: typified by St Augustine, this begins with the unity of God and works towards an understanding of the persons.

Modalism: a second-century theology that believed that the persons of the Trinity – Father, Son and Holy Spirit – were just roles played by one God.

Monism: the view that everything in the cosmos is made of one substance.

Monotheism: the belief, common to Judaism, Christianity and Islam, that there is only one God.

The 'ontological Trinity': the view – put forward, for example, by Origen – that the persons of the Trinity have the same being (*ousia*).

Perichoresis (a Greek word meaning 'going around', 'envelopment'): the idea that the persons of the Trinity 'dwell' mutually within one another.

Pluralism: the view that the cosmos is made up of different kinds of irreconcilable substance.

Polytheism: the belief that there are many gods.

The psychological analogy: proposed by St Augustine, this suggested that the persons of the Trinity can be compared to the unified state of mind of someone who is at once the agent of love (the lover), thinking of a love object (the beloved), and enacting the emotion of love.

The social analogy: the suggestion, dating from the Cappadocian Fathers, but depicted most famously in the Rublev Icon, that the Trinity consists of separate persons in society. The Rublev Icon shows the Trinity as three people sat around a table. Recent theologians (e.g. Moltmann, Pannenberg) have argued that we must begin with the persons of the Trinity and work towards an understanding of their unity.

Tritheism: belief in three gods, especially the doctrine that the three persons of the Trinity are three distinct Gods.

BOOKS

Colin Gunton, *The One, the Three and the Many* (CUP, 1993)

Catherine LaCugna, *God for Us: The Trinity and Christian Life* (HarperCollins, 1991)

The Truth

Religions offer their adherents 'truth', but the concept of 'truth' is extremely slippery and complex.

In ordinary language we use the word 'truth', apparently without much difficulty, to refer to those things which really are the case. This is the so-called 'correspondence' theory of truth, which regards a statement as truthful when it corresponds with 'the facts'. It is this version of 'truth' that gets tested in the courts. An accusation of murder is true only if the accused person actually committed the crime.

Advocates of the correspondence theory – from David Hume to the logical positivists and, lately, Richard Dawkins – have tended to be atheistic on the grounds that believers can never produce any indisputable divine 'facts' that could prove the claims of theology.

But this common-sense idea of truth assumes that the world consists of unambiguous 'facts' which can easily be produced or described. More often than not, 'the truth' must be interpreted from complex and ambiguous evidence. 'The causes of World War II', for example, are a matter of interpretation and debate, and we can imagine conflicting historical accounts being simultaneously true but in different ways. Furthermore, interpretations of the truth also change over time and between cultures.

It is this relationship between truth and historical/cultural change that has been at the heart of debates in philosophy and theology since the earliest times. Plato, for example, argued that truth occupies its own ideal world in which nothing ever changes. Karl Marx (following Hegel) argued that truth gets slowly realised in the changes of human history. The doctrine of the incarnation tries to embrace both these positions: The Truth is *both* a pure divine reality *and* living human history, *both* ideal knowledge *and* the process of existence. The incarnation also poses the problem of explaining how truth can be absolute and relative at the same time: how is God's timeless, cosmic idea of truth reconciled with Jesus' local expressions of truth in first-century Palestine? One solution is to imagine, as von Balthasar does, that truth is 'symphonic': a single reality composed of diverse parts playing themselves out over time.

Since the early twentieth century, and in particular the philosophy of Wittgenstein, some theologians have understand the word 'truth' as a purely cultural construct. So when I say X is 'true', this doesn't tell me anything about X, but only about my attitude to X. Thus it is not possible to speak about 'truth' as such, only about 'truth as we understand it'. More progressive 'post-modern' theologians, such as Don Cupitt, say that what we mean by 'truth' is always in flux and that there is no such thing as Truth in the abstract sense. This would mean that there is no 'symphony' of truth: only countless separate expressions.

We find the truth described in the Bible as a lived reality, an attitude to life or a path along which we must walk. Jesus describes himself as 'the way, the truth, and the life', which implies that truthfulness is much more than simply uttering true statements. The New Testament uses a very particular Greek word for truth – *aletheia*, or 'unforgetting' – which suggests that the truth is already within us and only needs to surface through layers of denial and forgetfulness.

THINKERS

Rudolf Bultmann (1884–1976) studied the concept of truth as *aletheia*, which is prominent in St John's Gospel: 'In John *aletheia* denotes "divine reality" with reference to the fact i) that this is different from the reality in which man first finds himself, and by which he is controlled, and ii) that it discloses itself and is thus revelation.'

Lord Byron (1788–1824) made the famous remark that 'truth is always strange;/ Stranger than fiction' (*Don Juan*).

Thomas Hobbes (1588–1679) argued the constructivist case that 'true and false are attributes of speech, not of things' (*Leviathan*).

John Keats (1795–1821) believed that 'Beauty is truth, truth beauty. That is all ye know, and all ye need to know.'

Søren Kierkegaard (1813–55) argued that 'subjectivity is truth, because the objective truth for an existing person is …

abstraction' (*Concluding Unscientific Postscript*).

Gotthold Lessing (1729–81) argued that the quest for truth was preferable to having the truth itself.

Friedrich Nietzsche (1844–1900) argued that truth is 'a movable host of metaphors, metonymies and anthropomorphisms: in short, a sum of human relations which have been poetically and rhetorically intensified, transferred and embellished, and which, after long usage, seem to people to be fixed, canonical and binding' (from 'On truth and lies in a non-moral sense').

Plato (c. 427–c. 347 BC) argued that truth derives from perfect and unchanging ideas (or 'forms') and that what is 'true' is also what is 'good'.

IDEAS

Aletheia: the Greek word for 'truth' used of and by Jesus, especially in John's Gospel.

Analytical truth: the truth of logic or mathematics – e.g. the truth that $2 + 2 = 4$ can be proven by logical analysis.

The coherence theory of truth argues that logically coherent statements are true.

The consensus theory of truth argues that the truth is what is agreed by consensus within a community or culture.

The constructivist theory of truth: the argument that truth is generated (constructed) by culture.

The correspondence theory of truth argues that true statements are those that correspond with the facts, or 'sense data', or states of affairs.

The deflationary theory of truth argues the 'minimal' or 'reductionist' case that all statements already contain implicit truth claims, so that saying that the statement 'God is good' is 'true', adds nothing to it, but merely restates the assertion 'God is good'. If the word 'true' doesn't do any work, it is therefore redundant.

The falsification principle: attributed to Karl Popper (1902–94), this states that a statement is meaningless if there is no way of falsifying it. If there is no way of falsifying belief in God, then such belief is empty.

The objective theory of truth: the argument that truth exists 'out there' independently of our subjective perceptions.

Perspectivism: the argument, put forward by Nietzsche, among others, that there is only the truth of our own particular perspective.

The pragmatic theory of truth argues that the truth is what works.

The subjective theory of truth: the argument that truth is only revealed in individual subjective experience.

The textualist theory of truth: the argument (put forward, for example, by the so-called structuralists) that truth always manifests itself within language.

Truth statements: according to Aristotle's logic, assertoric statements assert that something is the case (e.g. 'the grass is green'); problematic statements suggest a possible truth (e.g. 'it could rain tomorrow'); and apodictic statements present a self-evident truth (e.g. 'a triangle has three sides').

The verification principle argues that a statement is true when it can be verified from experience.

BOOKS

J. Richard Middleton and Brian J. Walsh, *Truth Is Stranger Than It Used to Be: Biblical Faith in a Postmodern Age* (InterVarsity Press, 1995)

Simon Blackburn and Keith Simmons, *Truth* (Oxford University Press, 1999)

Marcel Detienne, *The masters of truth in archaic Greece* (Zone Books, 1996)

Index of Names and Topics